MEL BAY PRESENTS

Christmas Favorites
for Solo Guitar

Best-Loved Traditional Songs for Bluegrass Guitar

by Dix Bruce

Special thanks to Marjorie McWee and Bob Bergman for their excellent suggestions.

Cover photo by Theresa Hioki.

CD CONTENTS

Table of Contents

Learn great flatpicking solos on 30 wonderful Christmas and Holiday tunes! Most solos use the basic "bass note/strum" technique with melodies integrated into common chord patterns. Others feature "the arpeggio strum," a beautiful chord melody technique. Along the way you'll explore transposing solos from one key to another, changing and mixing meter (3/4 to 4/4), soloing in more than one octave, playing a solo with others as a round, and more!

Introduction

I love Christmas music. I'm not sure exactly why, but it probably has to do with the warm memories of the holiday season that I have from my younger days. Christmas was a pretty big deal around our house, especially for the kids. Of course, I participated in all the holiday shows and pageants in the community, at church, and in school. Music was always the major part of the celebration and over the years I learned all the classics of the genre from traditional to popular.

As a musician, I'm often called upon to play Christmas music at a variety of events, parties, and get-togethers. The arrangements in this book reflect my experiences playing these classic songs for over forty years. I still enjoy playing them and hope you will too!

For beginning and intermediate guitarists

My aim was to make these solos playable by beginning and intermediate guitarists. Some will be downright simple to play, others a bit more challenging, but they're all doable with a little work. All the pieces in this book can be performed as a guitar solo or within a band context. I designed them to fit generally into a flatpicking/bluegrass guitar style both technique- and sound-wise. Of course, many of these melodies originated three to five hundred years ago and don't automatically lend themselves to a Bill Monroe or Flatt & Scruggs treatment. Some like "Jingle Bells," "Here We Come a'Caroling," and "Auld Lang Syne," are a natural fit for a bluegrassy sound. Others are perfect and quite beautiful in their more traditional settings. Call me old fashioned, but it didn't seem quite right to turn "O Come, O Come Emmanuel" or "Silent Night" into a foot stompin' breakdown. Still, these more traditional songs, chord progressions, and rhythms make beautiful guitar solos and will fit well into any musical context.

The solos and arrangements

I started out by arranging each song in a basic Carter-style where the melody note is played on the lower strings of the guitar and then that note is punctuated or answered with a strum on the upper strings. With this method one guitarist plays both rhythm and lead at the same time. It's an incredibly useful technique that is the basis of guitar playing in bluegrass, country, old-time, and folk music. "Carter-style" is named for the Carter Family's Maybelle Carter, probably the most influential guitarist in American music. Be sure to hold the chords shown whenever possible. Holding the chord will automatically take care of a lot of the fret fingerings. Some songs like "O Come, O Come Emmanuel" and "God Rest Ye Merry, Gentlemen" have passages of continual quarter or eighth notes with no room for strums. I tried to preserve the essential nature of each song and let it determine the arrangement.

Many of the solos include "arpeggio strum" passages. The "arpeggio strum" is similar to a technique known as "chord melody." With both "arpeggio strum" and "chord melody" we place the melody note on the highest pitched note of the chord. Then we arpeggiate, or play through the chord from the lowest pitched note to the highest pitched, sounding the individual notes of the chord. This technique gives us a beautifully arpeggiated chord backup plus the melody note. Similar to the Carter-style but with a totally different sound, it's like playing rhythm and lead at the same time. The "arpeggio strum" works well on the slower songs and you'll use it on "Away in a Manger," "The Coventry Carol," "The First Nöel," "I Saw Three Ships," "It Came Upon the Midnight Clear," and others.

Performing with singers

Since most of these songs are traditionally sung, I've listed typical vocal keys for males and females on each song. With that general information, you'll be able to play along with singers of all ranges. I used my own voice as a starting point. My voice is a fairly typical male voice, not too low, not too high. I have found that if I sing a song in the key of G, a typical female voice will sing the same song in the key of C or D, a fourth or fifth higher than where I sing it. This is reflected at the top left of each song and is noted as follows:

M: *G*, *F*: *C or D, capo 5 or 7*

"*M*" (in bold type): stands for "male voice," which will sing the song in the key of "G," "*F*" (in bold type): stands for "female voice," which will sing the song in the key of "C" or "D," when the chords shown in the music are capoed on guitar and played as suggested at fret 5 or 7. Obviously, you can locate the capo just about anywhere on the fingerboard and individual vocal ranges may require a capo adjustment one way or the other. As long as you have a capo, you can probably accommodate just about any voice.

I often refer to measure numbers in the introductions to the songs. Starting with the second staff of each piece, measure numbers are above and slightly to the left of the treble clef.

Many of the songs are pitched in the keys of G and C. There are several reasons for this. G and C are relatively easy guitar keys to play in and probably the most popular keys for folk, bluegrass, gospel, and old time music. However, all of the songs will fit well into other keys too. Don't be afraid to move them around. You'll discover all sorts of tonal characteristics unique to different keys. Later in the book we'll show you a couple of examples where we transpose from one key to another without the use of the capo. You'll see how easy it is to simply move a whole arrangement "over" one string to change the key from G to C, C to F, or from Em to Am. This knowledge, along with a capo, will allow you to play these arrangements in **any** key.

How to work with the book and CD

It's a good idea to listen to the recorded version of the song first to get an idea of how it goes. All the solos have been recorded at both slow and regular speed and are included on the CD. Track numbers for each song are shown after the vocal keys and in the alphabetical index on page fifty six. First try playing along with the slow speed version of a song on the recording. Gradually work your way up to the full speed version. All the songs are recorded in split-track stereo and you can adjust the balance of your player to hear either the lead or the rhythm or both. If you're listening on headphones, you can take one phone off and get the same effect. Guitar tuning tones are on track one of the CD.

I kept the rhythm backup on the recordings very simple, usually just strumming the chords. I played very few, if any, bass notes or runs. I did this deliberately so that my rhythm wouldn't compete with the lead guitar part. I play all the songs with a flatpick, but there's no reason you couldn't play them with your thumb and fingers or thumbpick and fingerpicks.

Hammer-ons, pull-offs, chord diagrams

Hammer-ons, noted in the music with a small italic "*h*," and pull-offs, noted in the music with a small italic "*p*," are shown between the standard notation and the tablature. Fretting finger suggestions are shown in the same area with small italic numbers. *1* = index, *2* = middle, *3* = ring, *4* = pinkie. If a solo requires special chord forms to play it, chord diagrams are shown in the song introduction preceding the music. An "x" under a string in a chord diagram means to not play that string. An "r" shows where the root of the chord is located.

I included one verse of lyrics to each song to help you find your way through the solos. You can download complete "E-Z to read" lyric sheets for holiday sing-alongs or further study from my website: http://www.musixnow.com/christmasguitardownloads.html.

Here's hoping you enjoy playing these great holiday songs and that they become a part of your holidays in the years to come. Oh, and Merry Christmas!

—*Dix Bruce*

Dix Bruce is a musician and writer from the San Francisco Bay Area. He has authored over fifty books, recordings, and videos for Mel Bay Publications. Dix performs and does studio work on bass, guitar, mandolin, and banjo. He has recorded two LPs with mandolin legend Frank Wakefield, eight big band CDs with the Royal Society Jazz Orchestra, his own collection of American folk songs entitled "My Folk Heart" on which he plays guitar, mandolin, autoharp and sings; and a CD of string swing and jazz entitled "Tuxedo Blues." He has released four CDs of traditional American songs and originals with guitarist Jim Nunally, most recently a collection of "brother duet" style recordings entitled "Brothers at Heart." Dix arranged, composed, and played mandolin on the soundtracks to four different editions of the best selling computer game "The Sims." For a listing of Dix's publications, see page 53 or log onto his website: **www.musixnow.com**.

photo by Theresa Hioki

Dix Bruce

Silent Night

M: G, F: C or D, capo 5 or 7, CD Tracks 2 & 3

Grüber, Möhr, 1818

"Silent Night" is probably the best loved Christmas song ever. It's beautiful, peaceful, and easy to play and sing. I've included lots of hammer-ons to give it a Carter-style sound. Be sure to play "Silent Night" at a slow and even tempo that vocalists would choose. Don't hurry it.

Arrangement copyright © 2009 by Dix Bruce

Away in a Manger

M: G, F: C or D, capo 5 or 7, CD Tracks 4 & 5 *Mueller, 19th century*

G

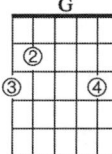

"Away in a Manger" is one of my favorites. It's so sweet and innocent. You'll use the "arpeggio strum" technique extensively in this arrangement. To play an arpeggio strum, hold the chord shown and drag through the strings, lowest to highest pitched, sounding each individually but allowing the last note, the melody note, to sound louder than the others. Check it out on the recording. The G chord at left is used in measures one and nine.

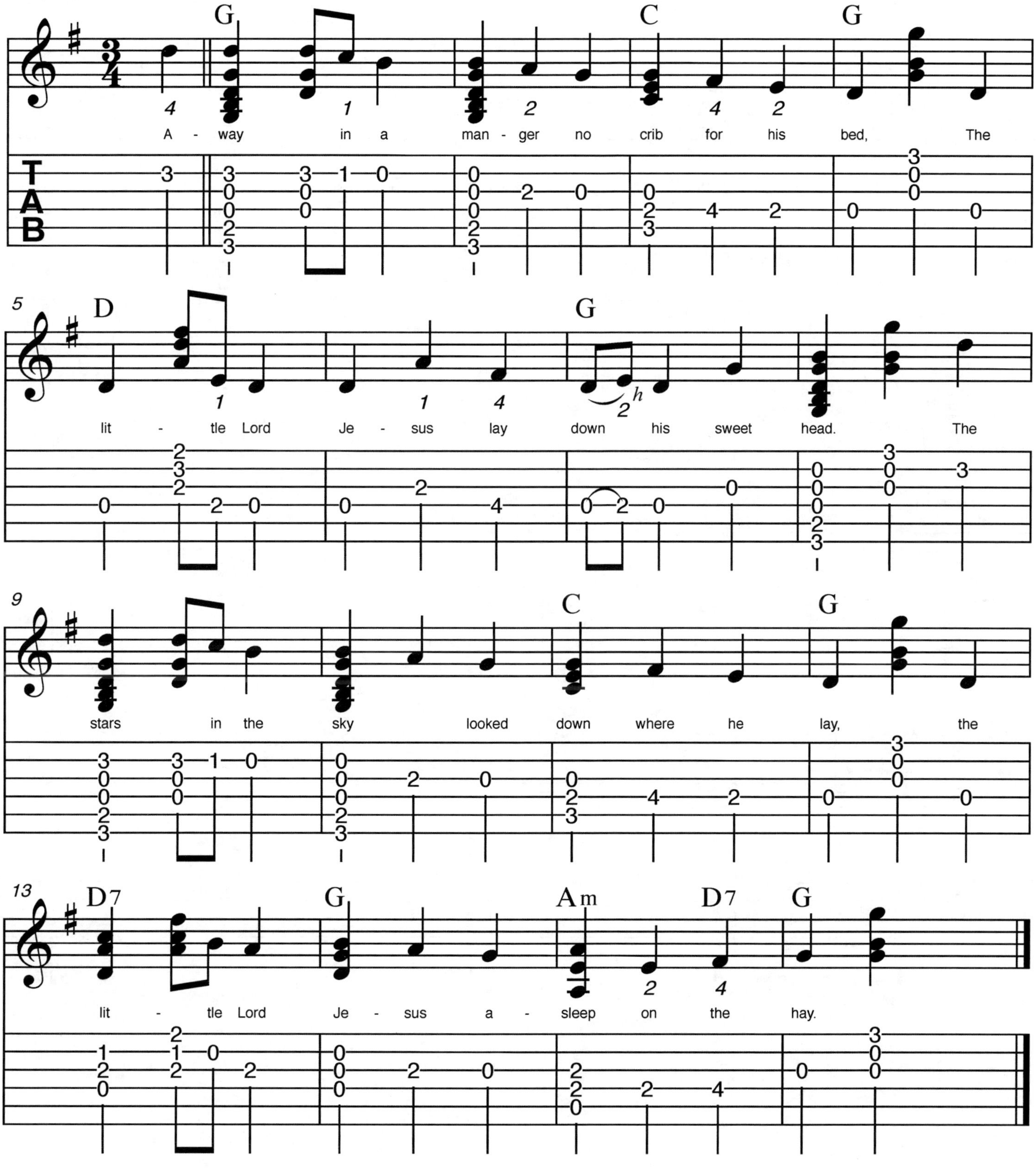

G C G
A - way in a man - ger no crib for his bed, The
D G
lit - tle Lord Je - sus lay down his sweet head. The
C G
stars in the sky looked down where he lay, the
D7 G Am D7 G
lit - tle Lord Je - sus a - sleep on the hay.

Joy to the World

M: C, F: F or G, capo 5 or 7, CD Tracks 6 & 7 *Handel, Watts, 18th Century*

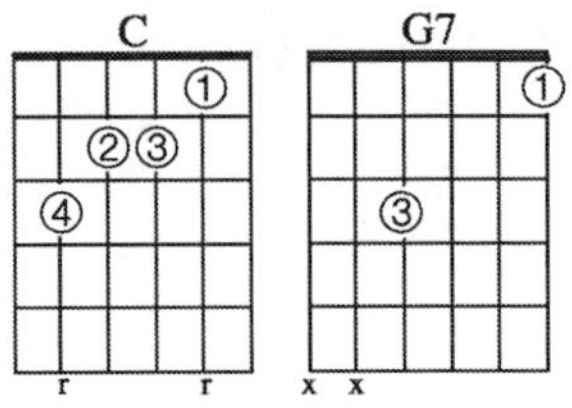
C
G7

This arrangement of "Joy to the World," another of the greatest hits of Christmas music, is a mixture of routine flatpicking (with various hammers and one pull-off in measure sixteen) and the arpeggio strum (measures one, two, seven, eight, etc.). "Joy to the World" works well at a variety of speeds but I prefer it at a slower tempo. You'll use the modified C chord at left in measures nine and eleven.

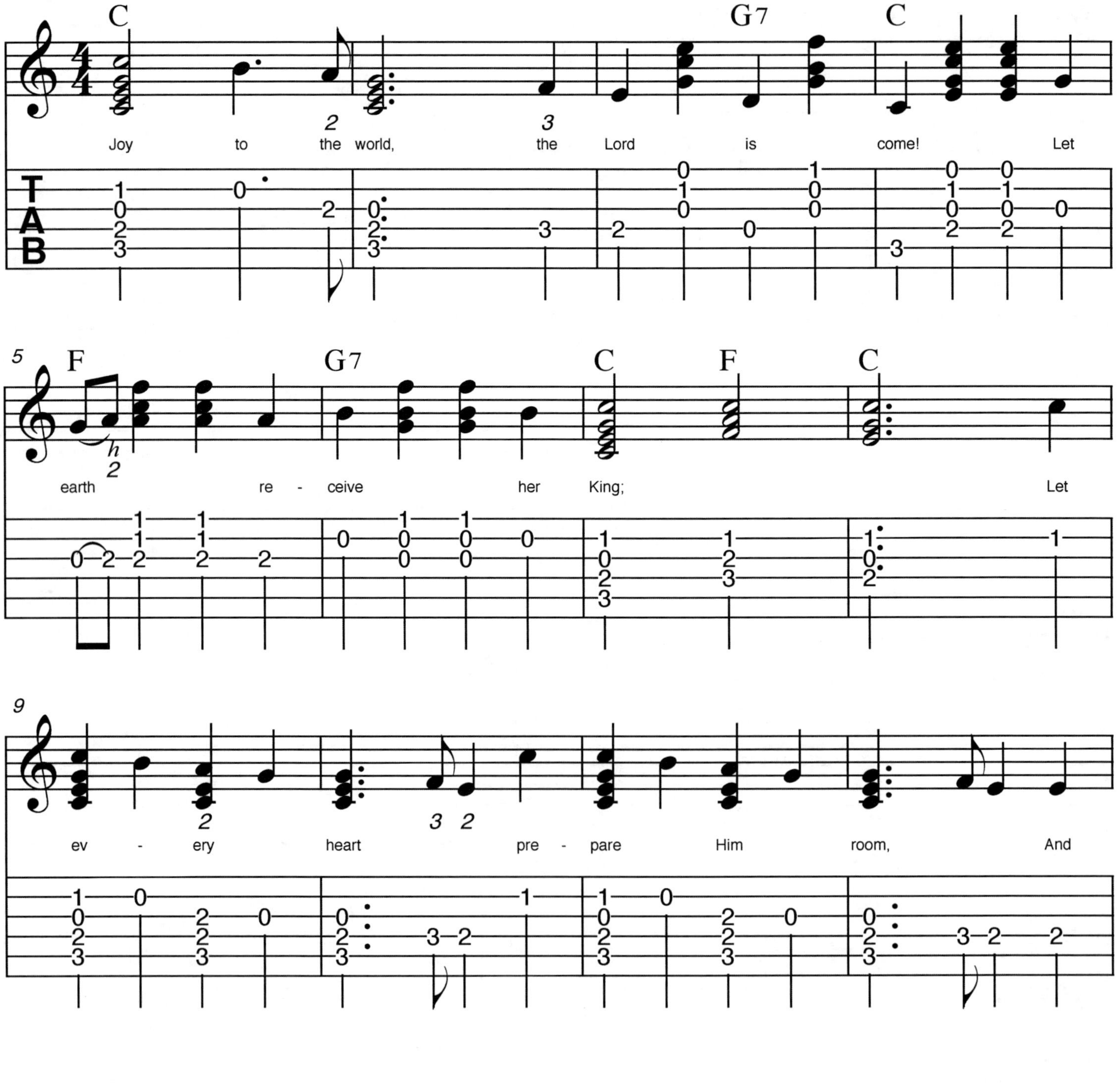
C G7 C
Joy to the world, the Lord is come! Let
F G7 C F C
earth re - ceive her King; Let
ev - ery heart pre - pare Him room, And

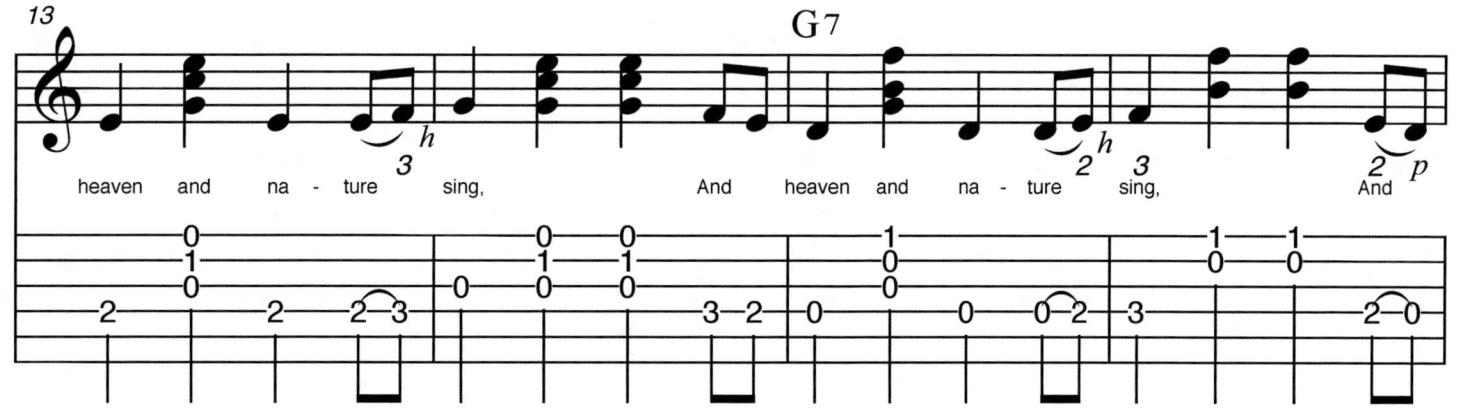

heaven and na - ture sing, And heaven and na - ture sing, And

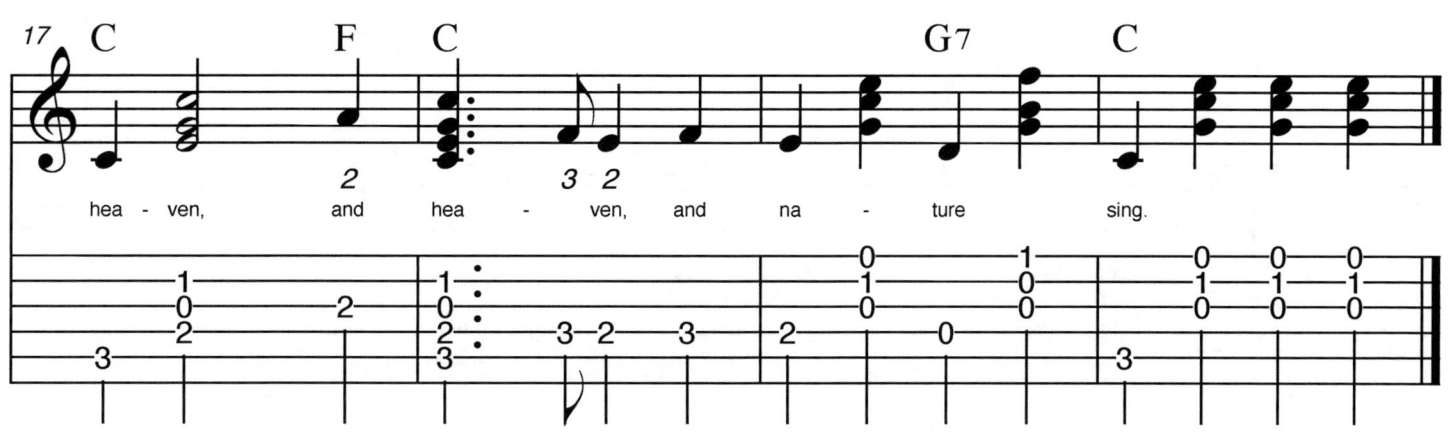

hea - ven, and hea - ven, and na - ture sing.

Jingle Bells

M: G, capo 7, F: C or D, capo 0 or 2, CD Tracks 8 & 9

Pierpont, 1857

"Jingle Bells" is everybody's favorite winter song. Play it hot and fast once you've learned it and don't forget the hammers!

Angels We Have Heard on High

M: C, F: F or G, capo 5 or 7, CD Tracks 10 & 11

Traditional

"Angels We Have Heard on High" includes lots of hammers to give it a real bluegrass or Carter-style sound. Hold the chords shown as you play through the solo and most of the note fingerings will be made for you. The 1/8 notes in measures five through seven may be a challenge. I use down pick strokes on notes that fall on the beat, upstrokes on notes that fall on the "ands" between beats. If you have difficulty with the pull off in measure five, leave it out for now. The Dm shown at left will come in handy in measure six.

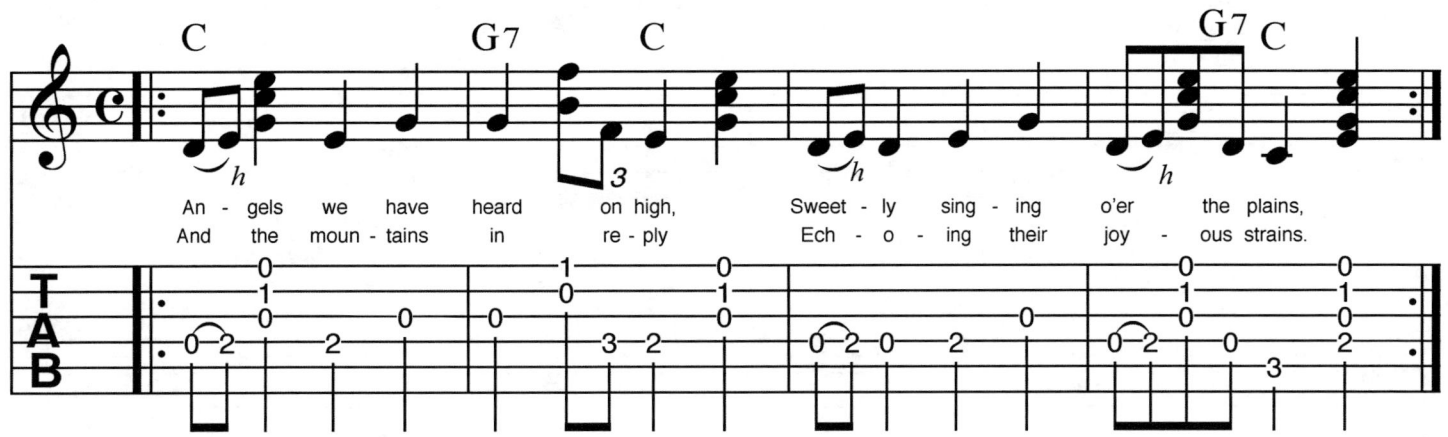

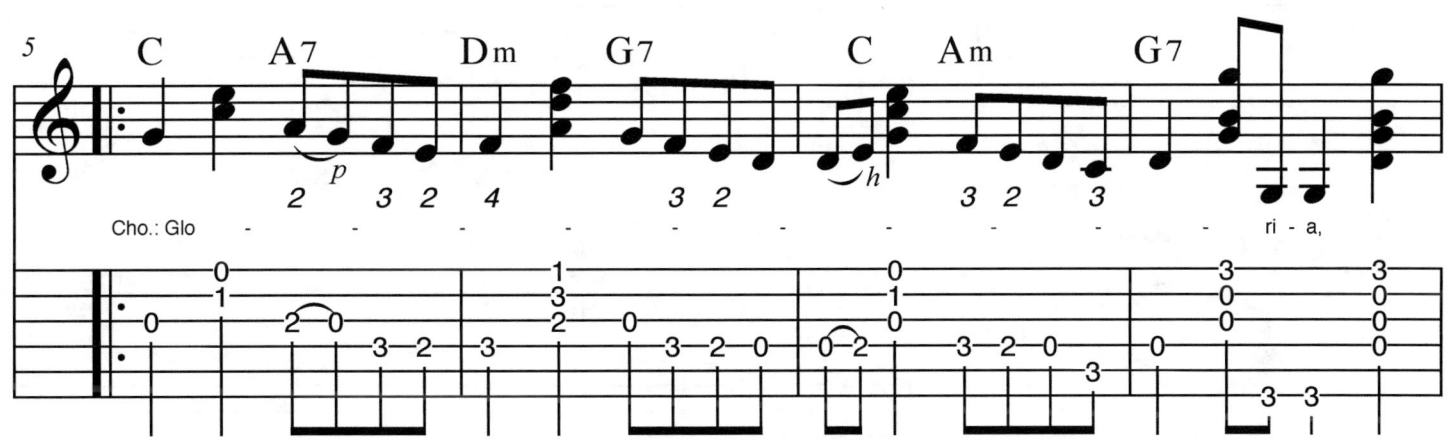

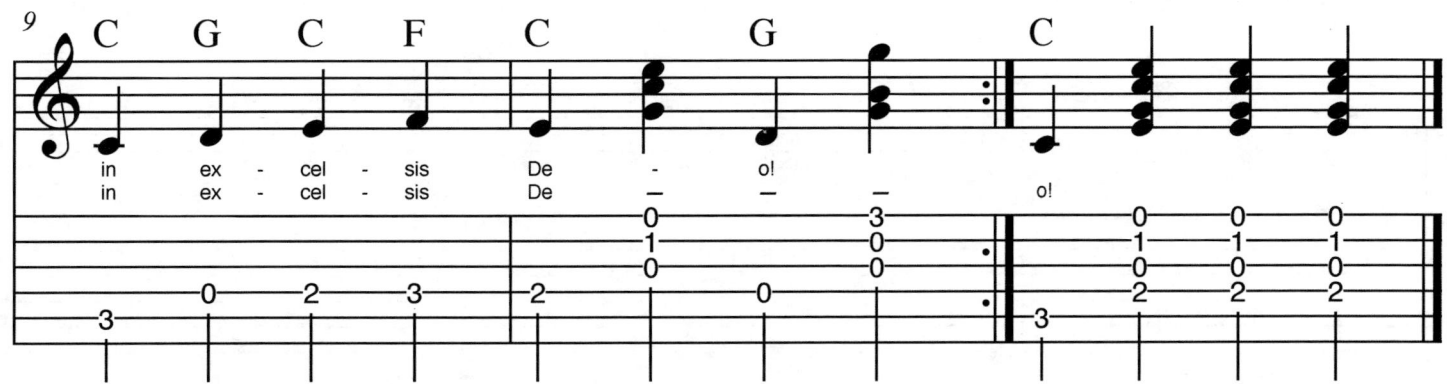

Go Tell It on the Mountain

M: G, capo 7, F: C or D, capo 0 or 2, CD Tracks 12 & 13

Work, 19th century

Once you get the hang of it, play this bluegrassy solo fast. It has lots of hammers and a pull-off in measure twelve. Experiment with a *ritard* or gradual slowing in measure eight. Try pulloffs on some of the eighth notes in measure nine.

Jolly Old St. Nicholas

M: G, capo 7, F: C or D, capo 0 or 2, CD Tracks 14 & 15

Traditional

You'll use the Am chord in measure three, the E7 in ten, the C in the last measure. If you have difficulty with the last C chord, you can substitute any other C. Measures one and two are repeated in measures nine and ten except that I substituted the E7 chord for the G to change the progression a bit. Otherwise, it's pretty straight forward flatpicking throughout.

The First Nöel

M: C, F: F or G, capo 5 or 7, CD Tracks 16 & 17

English carol, 18th century

Another of the greatest hits on traditional Christmas music. I'd always heard it was from the French tradition but lately conventional wisdom says it's from the English. French or English, it's a beautiful song.

Children Go Where I Send Thee

M: *D, capo 2,* **F: G***, capo 7, CD Tracks 18 & 19*

African-American

"Children Go Where I Send Thee" is a gospel, bluegrass, and country Christmas standard. The bass runs at the beginning and end give it a nice hot-flatpicked guitar flavor. If the eighth notes in measure seven give you trouble, leave out every other one and play them as quarters. As succeeding verses of the song are sung, it gains measures as in "The Twelve Days of Christmas." Try a pull-off instead of the hammer-on on beat one of measure six.

Deck the Hall

M: D, capo 7, F: A or B, capo 2 or 4, CD Tracks 20 & 21

Welsh traditional

"Deck the Hall" (or "Deck the Halls") is always energetic and fun. You'll get a chance to play it here in two octaves in the key of G. Some of the chord changes comes quickly in measures eight and twenty. Your accompanist may choose to leave out the A7.

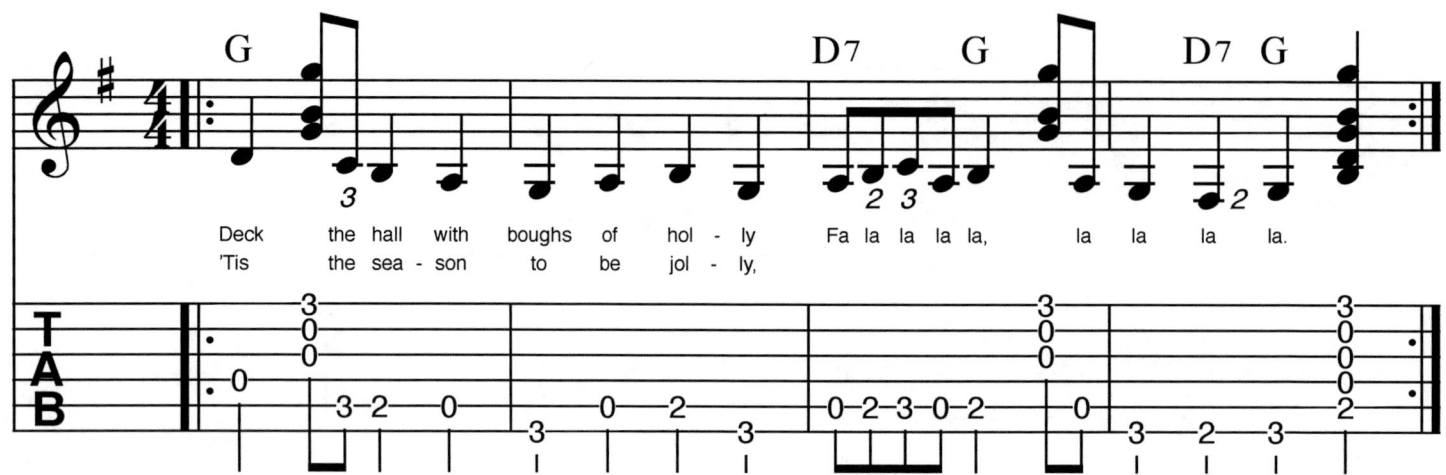

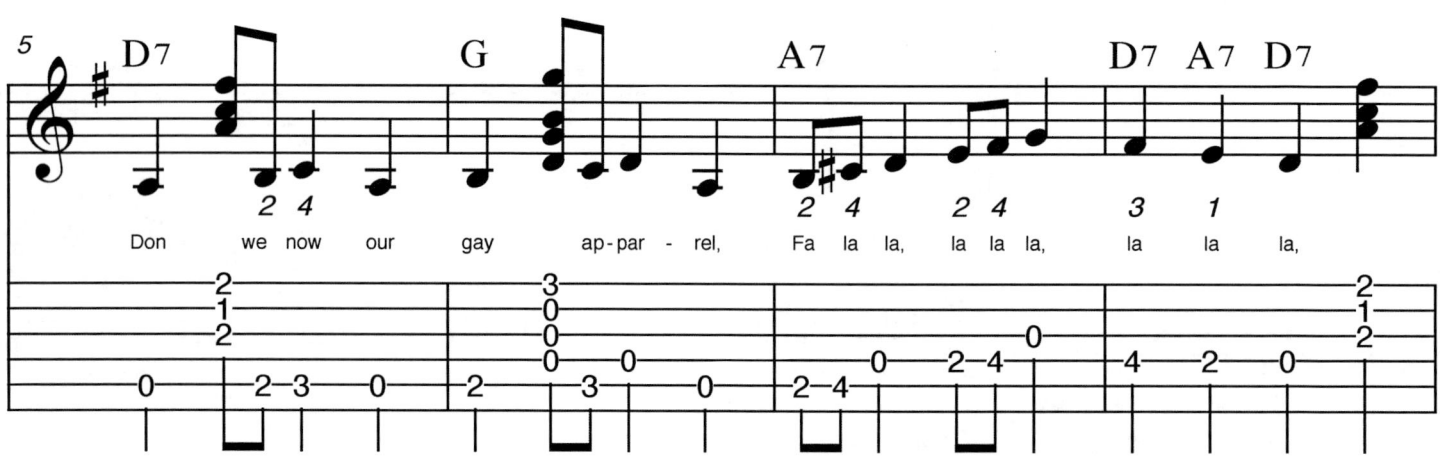

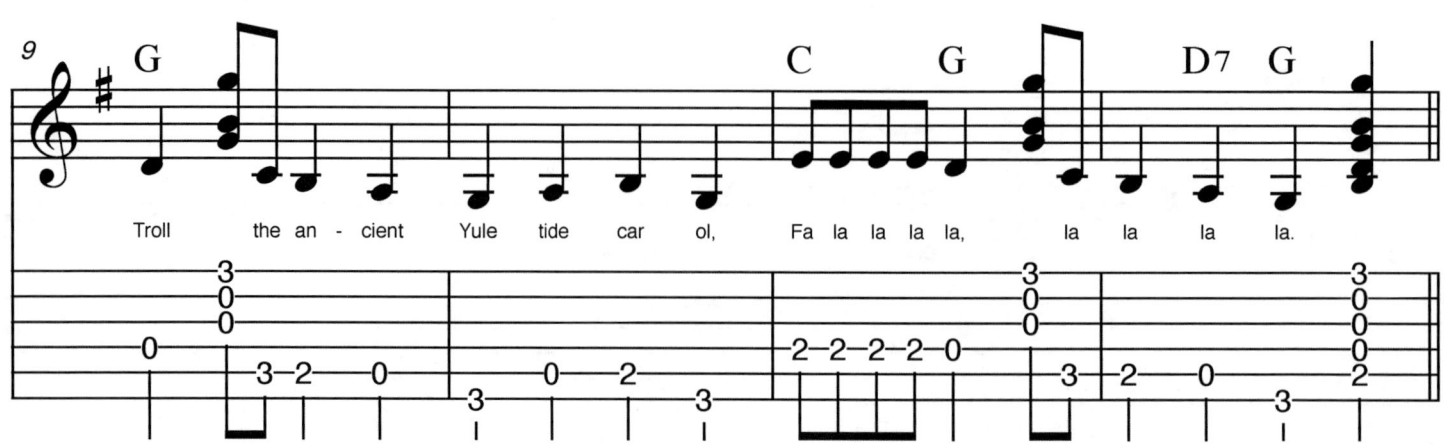

Arrangement copyright © 2009 by Dix Bruce

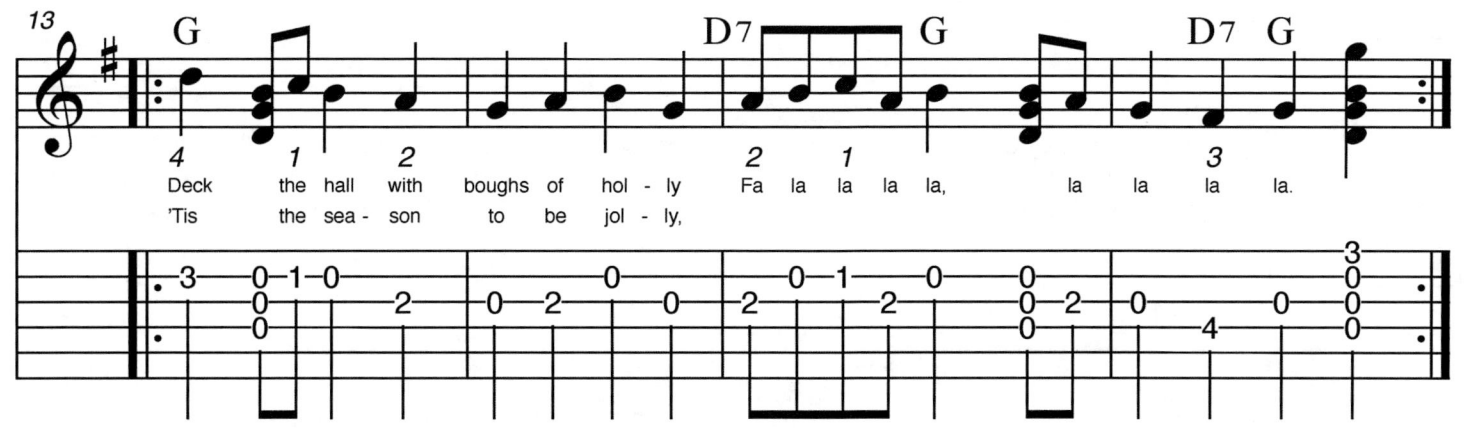

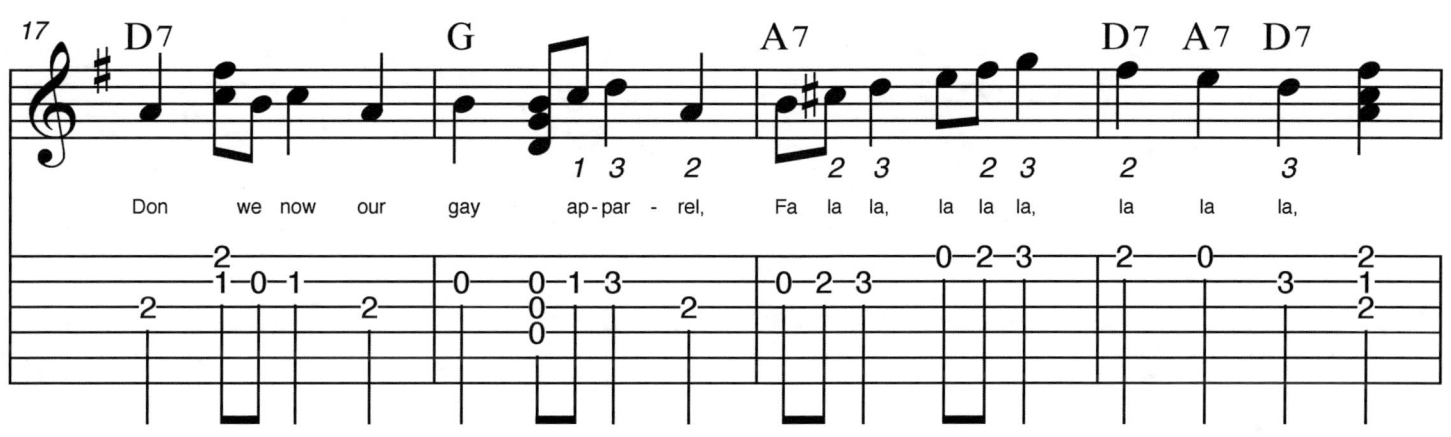

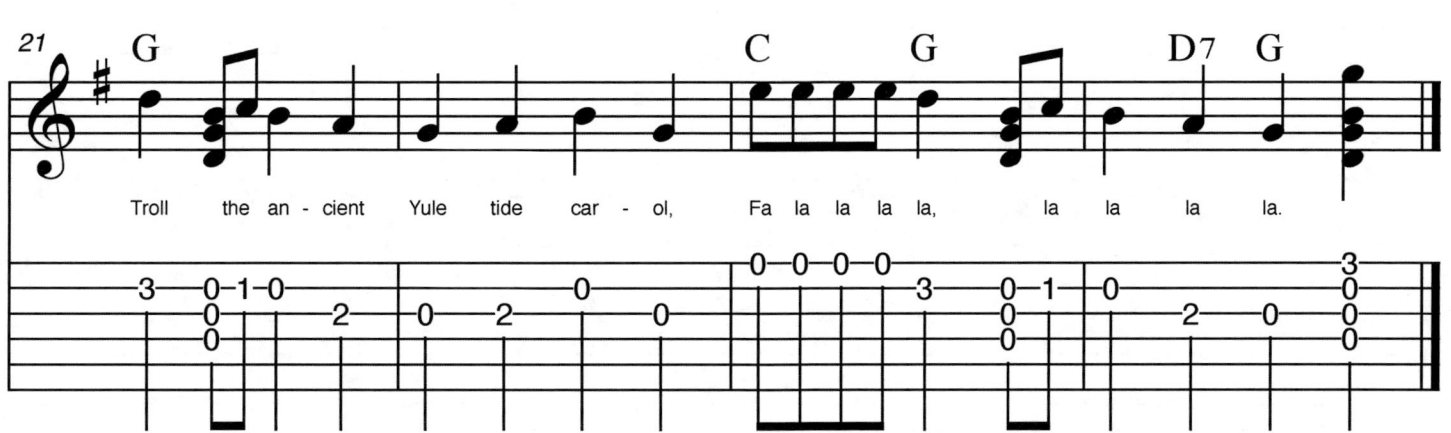

O Come, O Come Emmanuel

M: Am, F: Dm or Gm, capo 5 or 7, CD Tracks 22 & 23

Gregorian chant, 8th Century

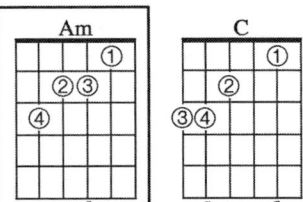

Since the melody to "O Come, O Come Emmanuel" has so many quarter notes and so few strums, it's good to have a rhythm guitarist back you up on this one. The feel of the song is so wonderfully minor and dark — wintery, I guess. Try adding some in and see if you like the effect. You'll need the Am throughout and the C in measure nine. I deliberately left out any possible hammers to preserve that feel.

Arrangement copyright © 2009 by Dix Bruce

Here We Come A'Caroling

"Here We Come A'Caroling," also known as "Here We Come A'Wassailing" is traditionally performed in mixed meter. The verse ("Here we come a'caroling among the leaves so green") has a three or 3/4 feel while the chorus ("Love and joy come to you") has a two (2/4) or four (4/4) feel. It's this meter change that gives the song its unique character.

I changed "Here We Come A'Caroling" by stretching it out and setting the whole thing, verse and chorus, to a 4/4 feel. I added strums after most melody notes to double the number of measures each melodic phrase takes up. This is a typical musical trick to bring a non-bluegrass song into the bluegrass realm. A five string banjo would fit perfectly into this arrangement. The bass note walkup at the beginning and the hammers scattered throughout give it a bluegrassy sound. The song itself has some very interesting chord changes beginning in measure twenty four with the Em to C to A to F passage.

Here We Come A'Caroling

M: C, F: F or G, capo 5 or 7, CD Tracks 24 & 25

Traditional English

Christmas Favorites for Solo Guitar by Dix Bruce

Arrangement copyright © 2009 by Dix Bruce

O Come all Ye Faithful

M: G, capo 7, F: C or D, capo 0 or 2, CD Tracks 26 & 27

Wade, 18th Century

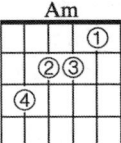

"O Come All Ye Faithful" comes from the Latin "Adeste Fideles" and it's one of the most loved Christmas songs. I stretched the meter of the piece and stressed the backbeats to give it more of a country and bluegrass feel. You'll need the Am form shown in measure nine.

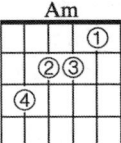

Hey Ho, Nobody Home

M: Dm, F: Gm or Am, capo 5 or 7, CD Tracks 28 & 29   *Traditional English*

"Hey Ho, Nobody Home" has a wonderful Dm/modal sound. The solo is fairly easy to play. Once you can play it from memory, get together with some musician friends and try playing it as a round, three or four times through. I recorded it as a round on the up-to-speed example on the CD. The first person starts at measure one. The second person starts at measure one when the first person reaches measure three, shown below with a single asterisk (*). The third person starts when the first person reaches measure five, shown below with two asterisks (**).

With its of its relative simplicity, "Hey Ho, Nobody Home" is a good song to practice transposing. Because of the way the guitar is tuned, we can often move a melody "over" and down or up in pitch to an adjacent set of strings and to a new key. Once you can play it as written from memory in Dm modal, try moving the whole solo "over" one string so that your first note is the open fifth string A. Change the Dm chords to Am, C chords to G, Em to Bm, and the F to a C. The new key will be Am modal. If you'd like to download a copy of the music in Am modal, visit my website: http://www.musixnow.com/christmasguitardownloads.html. Try this type of "one string over" transposing on other songs in this book. Start with "Silent Night" on page six.

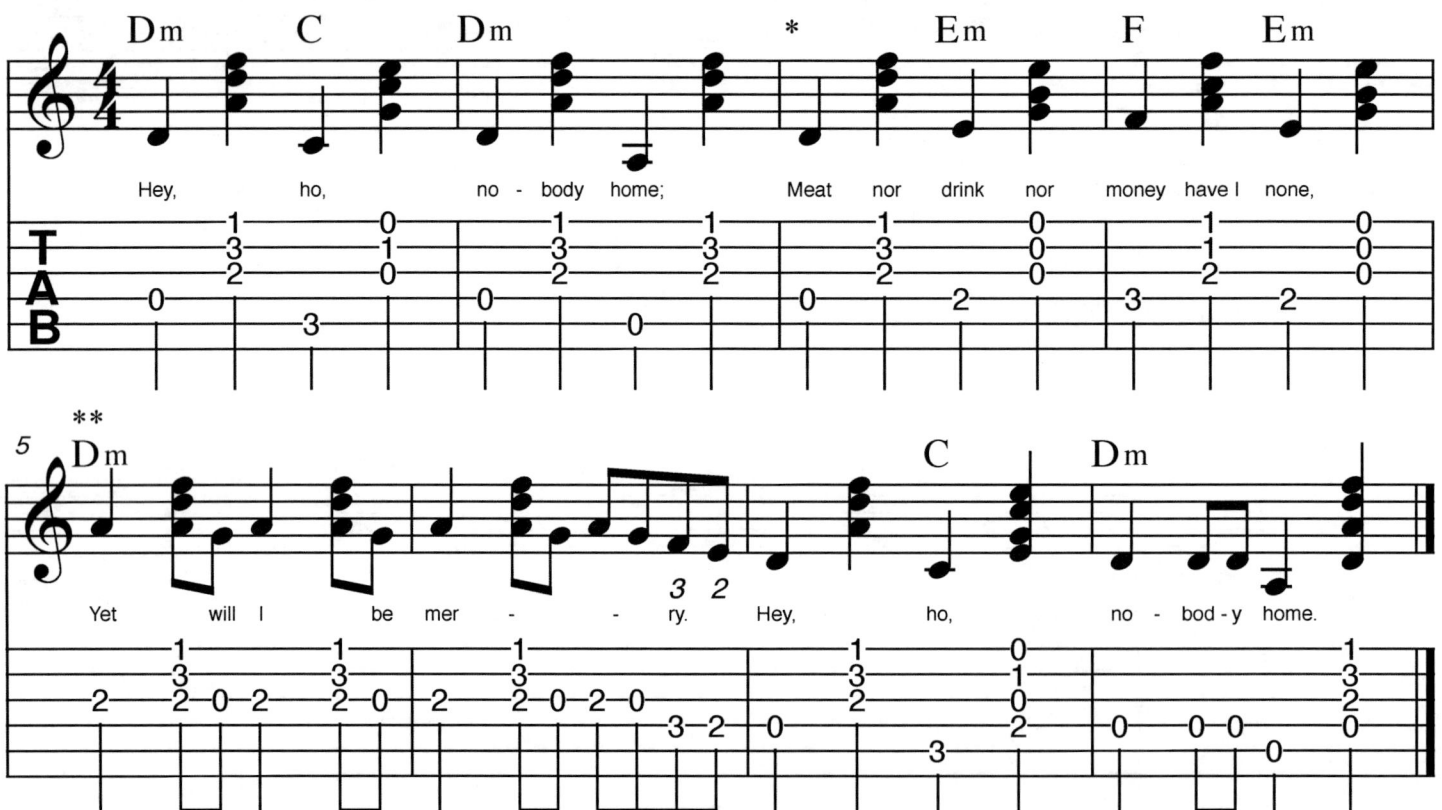

* = Part 2 begins when part 1 reaches here
** = Part 3 begins when part 1 reaches here

Arrangement copyright © 2009 by Dix Bruce

Good King Wenceslas

*M: G, capo 7, **F**: C or D, capo 0 or 2, CD Tracks 30 & 31*

Traditional, 18th century

The melodic structure of "Good King Wenceslas" makes it a good candidate for a hot, bluegrassy solo in the key of C.

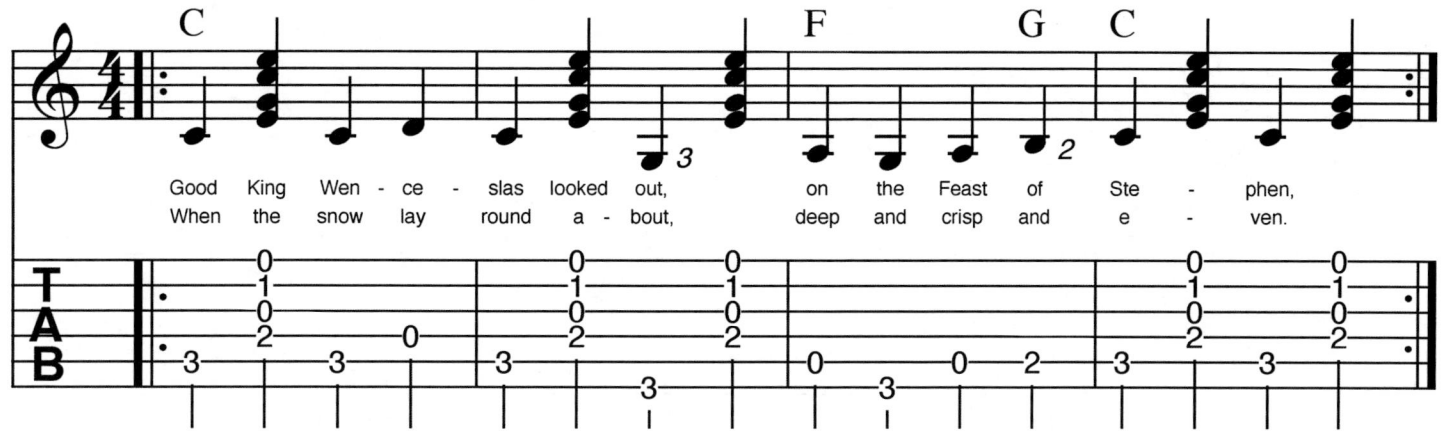

Good King Wen - ce - slas looked out, on the Feast of Ste - phen,
When the snow lay round a - bout, deep and crisp and e - ven.

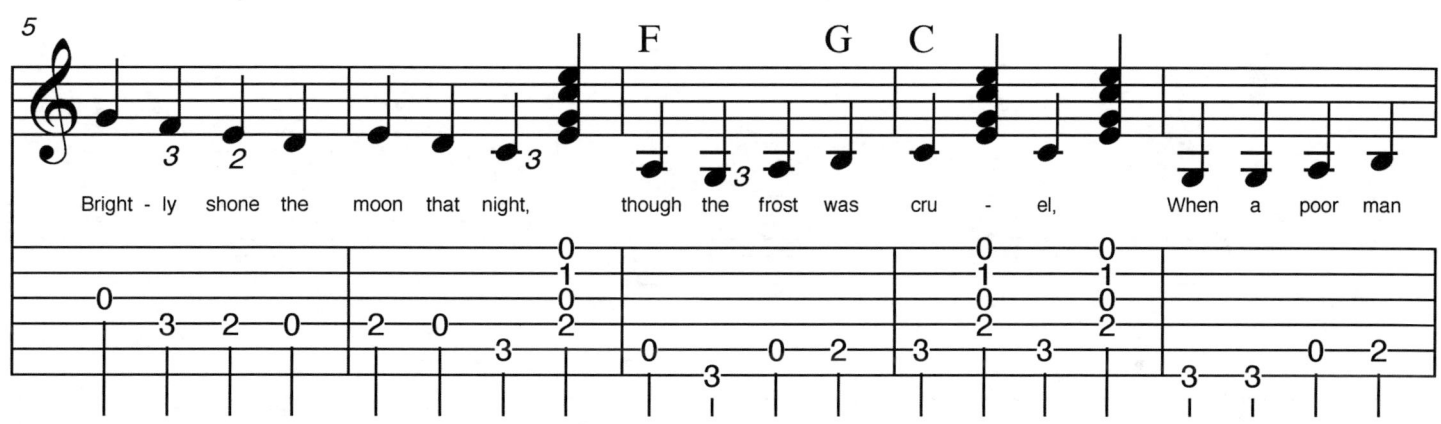

Bright - ly shone the moon that night, though the frost was cru - el, When a poor man

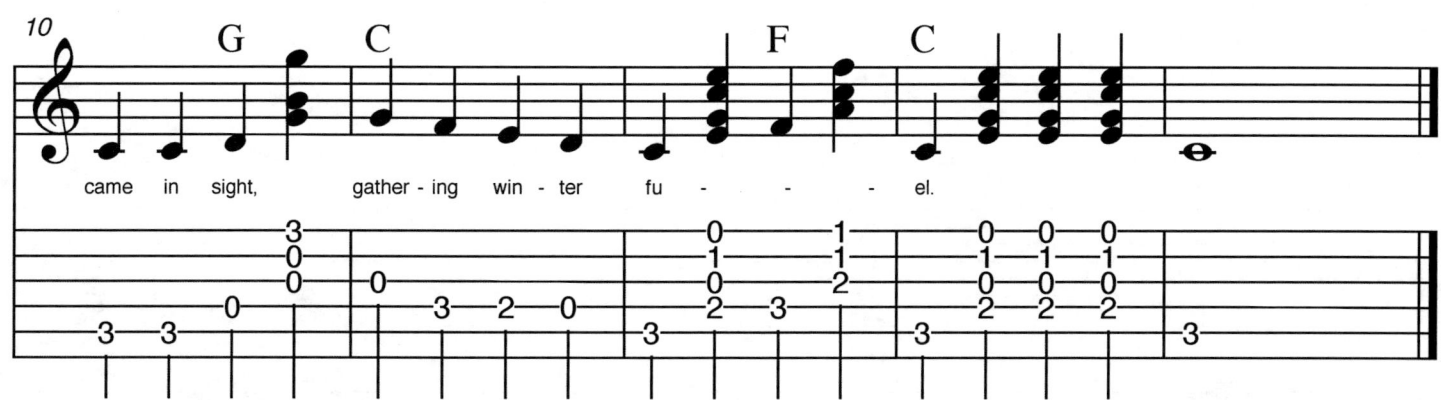

came in sight, gather - ing win - ter fu - - - el.

Bring a Torch, Jeanette, Isabella

M: *F, capo 5,* **F:** *C or D, capo 0 or 2, CD Tracks 32 & 33*

French, 17th Century

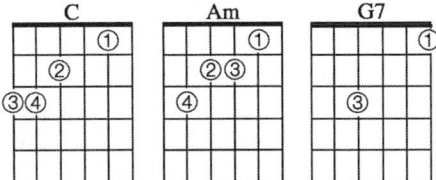

"Bring a Torch" is not as well known as some of the other songs in this book, but I think it's a great addition to anyone's holiday repertoire. Use the full C in measure fourteen, the Am in measures seventeen, and twenty two, and the partial G7 in measure fifteen.

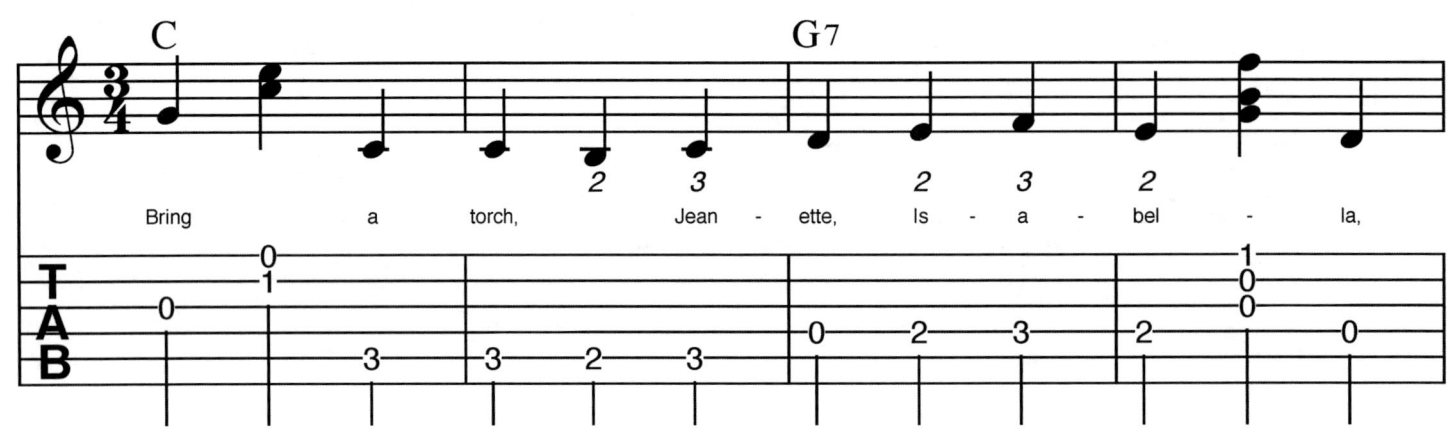

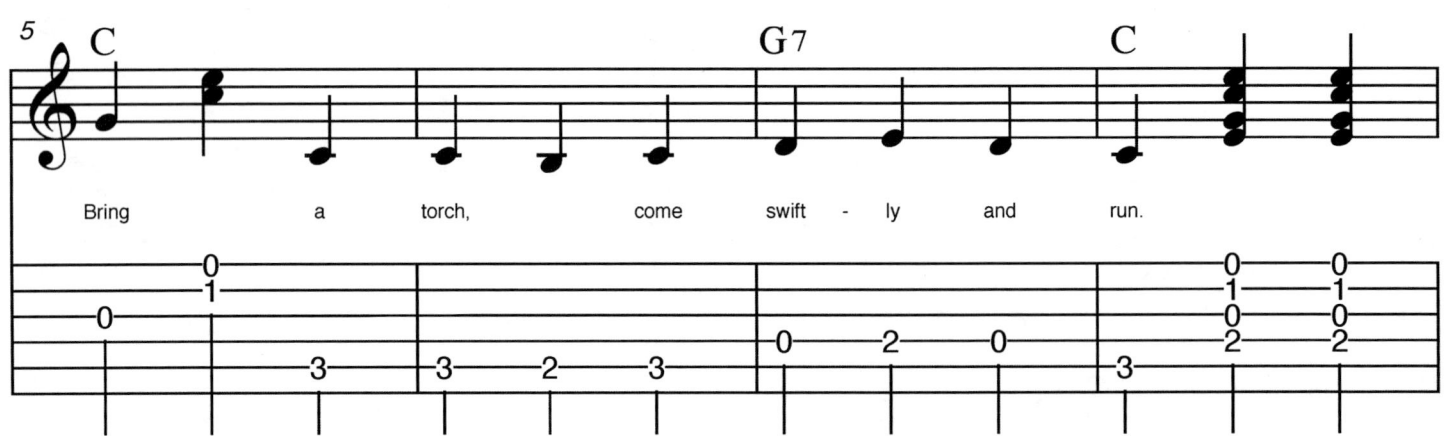

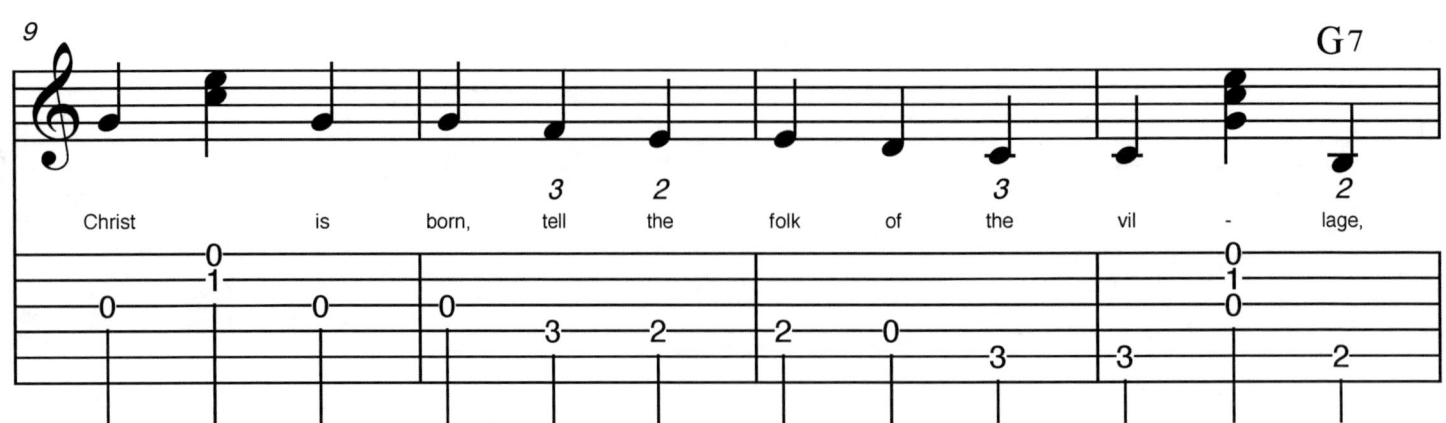

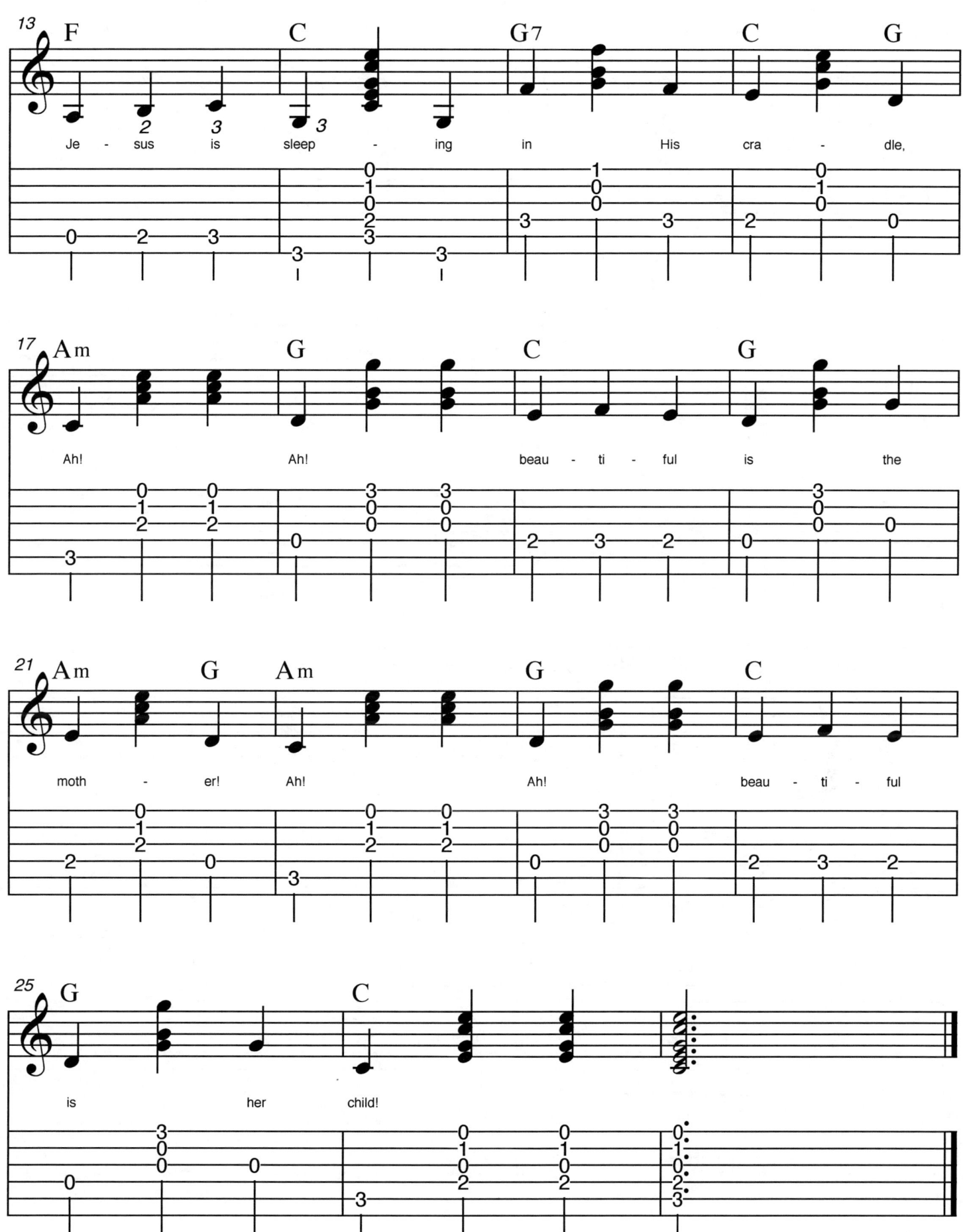

Ding Dong Merrily on High

M: G, F: C or D, capo 5 or 7, CD Tracks 34 & 35

Traditional, 16th century

Note the resemblance of the "gloria" melody in measures nine through fourteen with measures nine through twelve of "Angels We Have Heard on High" (page eleven). Try repeating measures five through twelve to lengthen the arrangement.

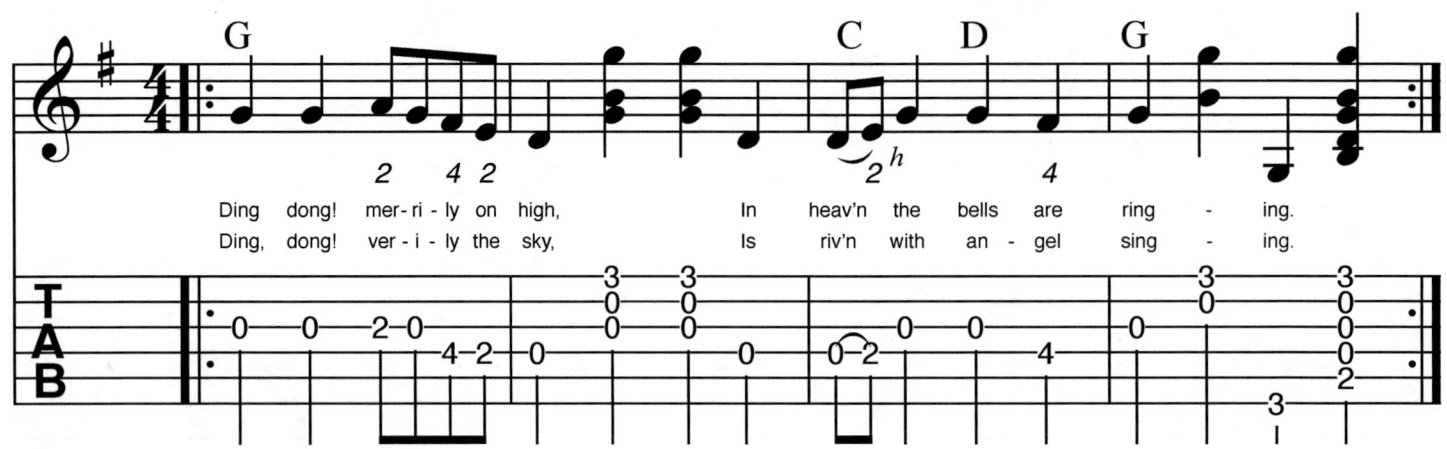

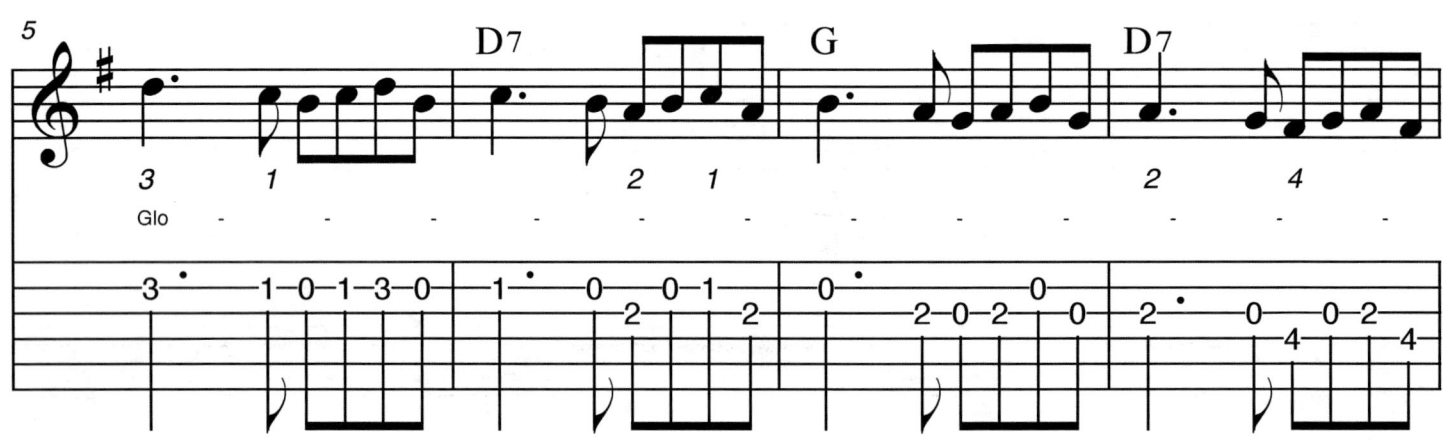

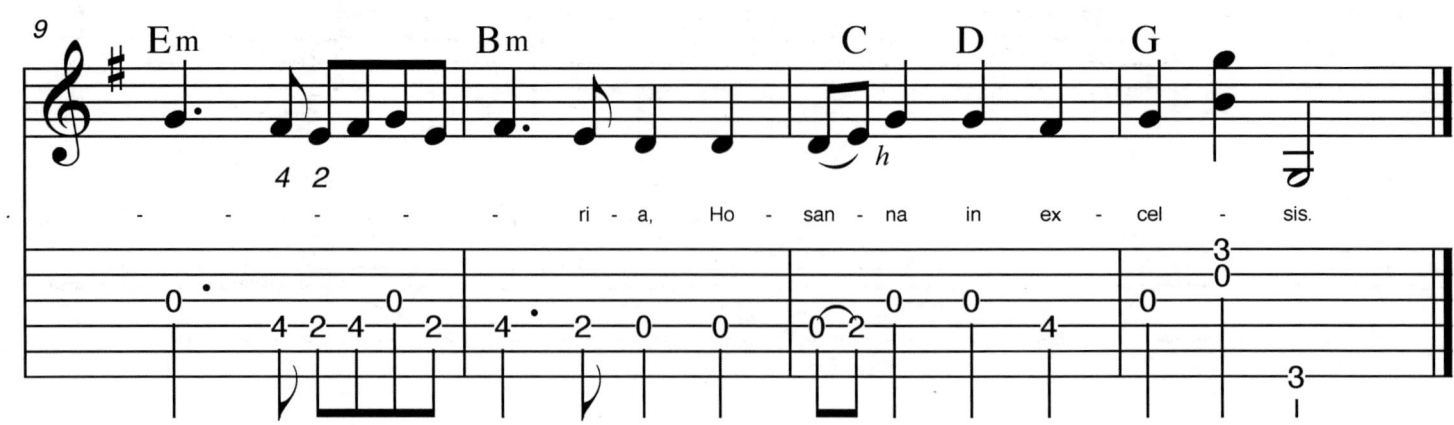

Rise Up, Shepherds, and Follow

M: C, F: F or G, capo 5 or 7, CD Tracks 36 & 37

African American

"Rise Up, Shepherds, and Follow" is straight flatpicking from top to bottom. It has a bluesier feel than most Christmas songs and has some actual blues notes, the Bbs, in measures three and eleven. To lengthen this arrangement, repeat the first eight measures.

O Christmas Tree

M: *C, capo 2 ,* **F:** *F or G, capo 5 or 7, CD Tracks 38 & 39*

Traditional German, 19th century

"O Christmas Tree" or "O Tannenbaum" is usually performed in 3/4 or 6/8. I decided to change the meter to 4/4 to give it a peppy, robust, bluegrassy/flatpick feel. I'm hoping those traditional Germans won't mind.

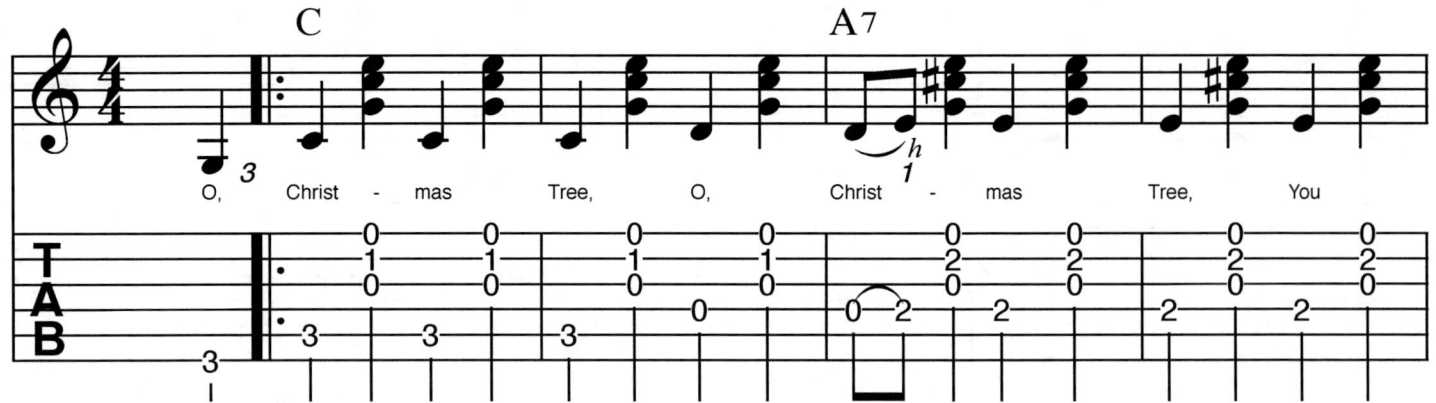

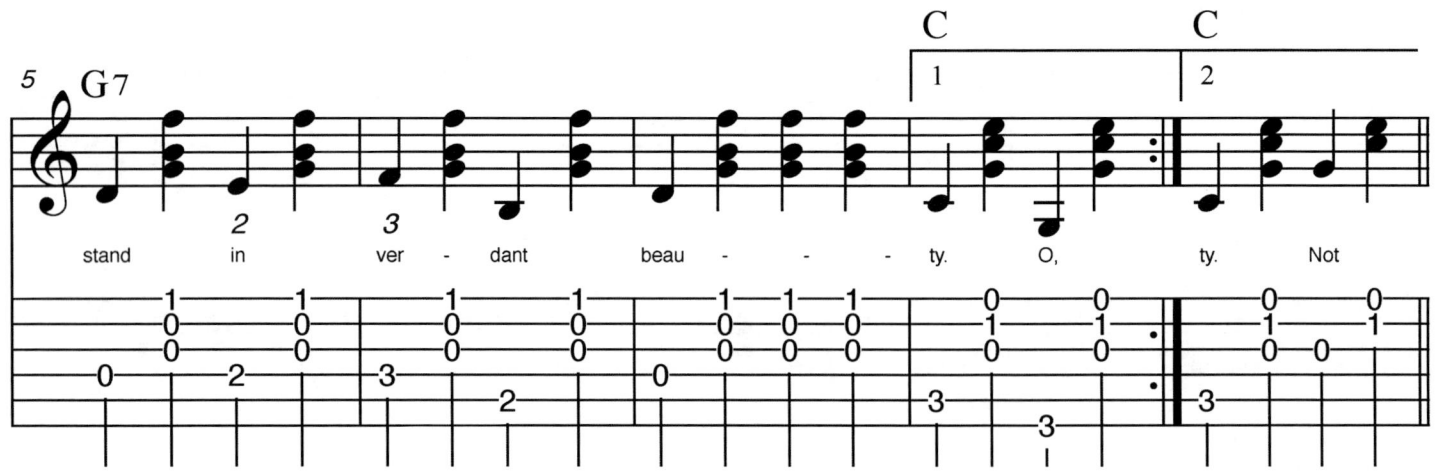

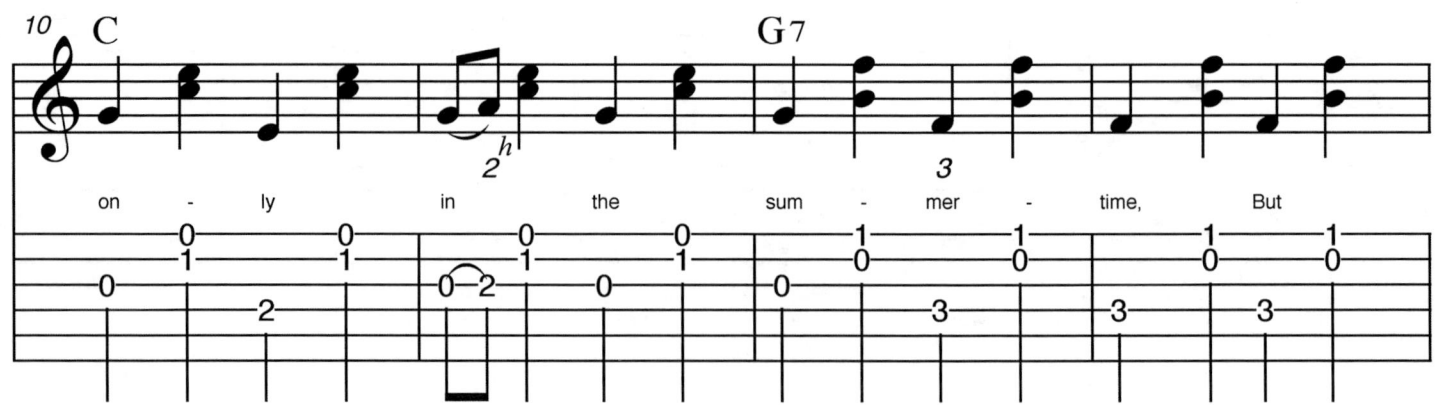

Arrangement copyright © 2009 by Dix Bruce

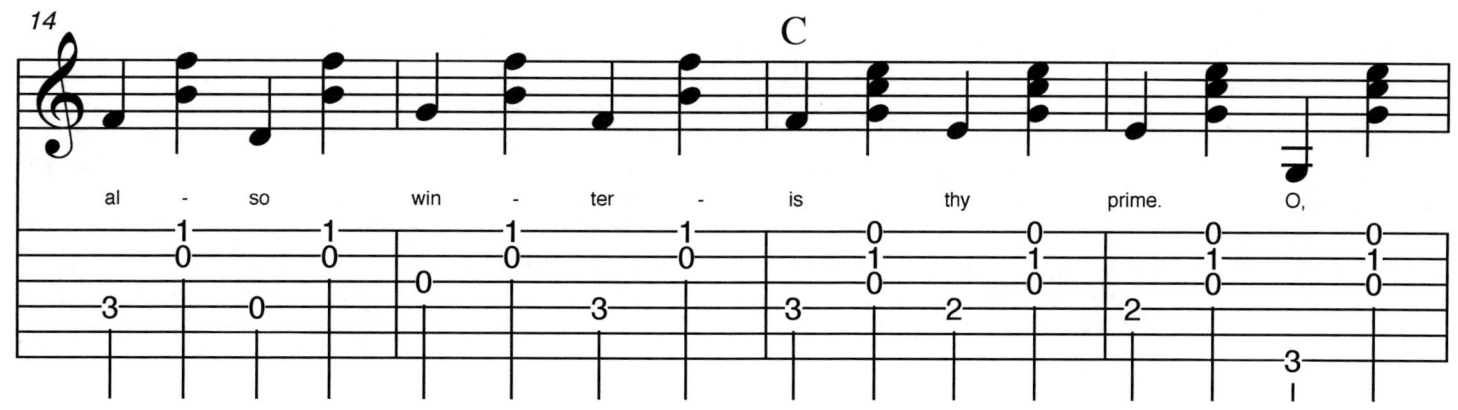

al - so win - ter - is thy prime. O,

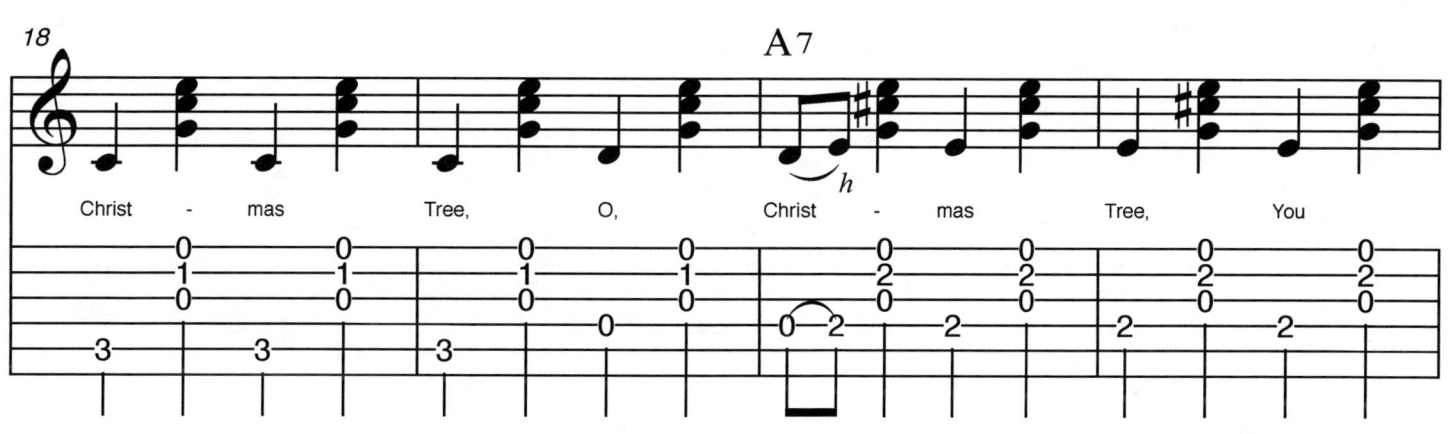

Christ - mas Tree, O, Christ - mas Tree, You

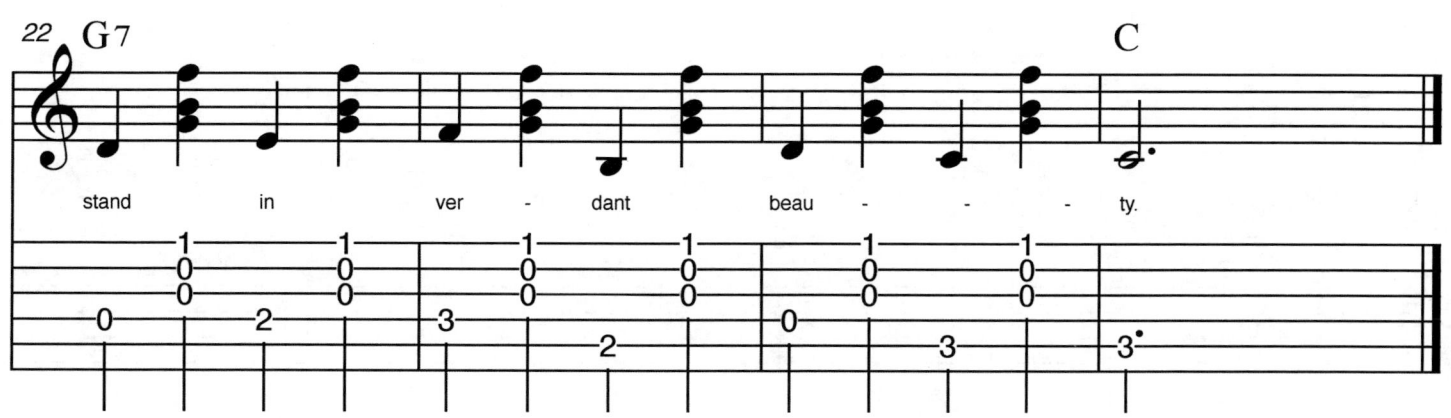

stand in ver - dant beau - - ty.

I Saw Three Ships

M: C, F: F or G, capo 5 or 7, CD Tracks 40 & 41

Traditional English, 17th century

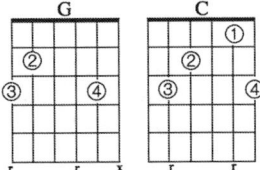

Many traditional songs are set in 3/4 or 6/8 time. 3/4 is also called waltz time and 6/8 is a variation of 3/4. I thought it might be interesting to experiment with the meter of "I Saw Three Ships" in both 3/4 to 4/4. The first part of "I Saw Three Ships" is in 3/4, the traditional setting, the second is in 4/4. See which you like best. Use the arpeggio strum on the half notes in measures one through sixteen. With arpeggio strums, the melody note is placed on the highest string of the chord. Drag through and play the chord, lowest to highest, across the strings but emphasize the highest or melody note of the chord more than the others. Diagrams for the G and C chords in part one are shown at left.

Part 1: 3/4

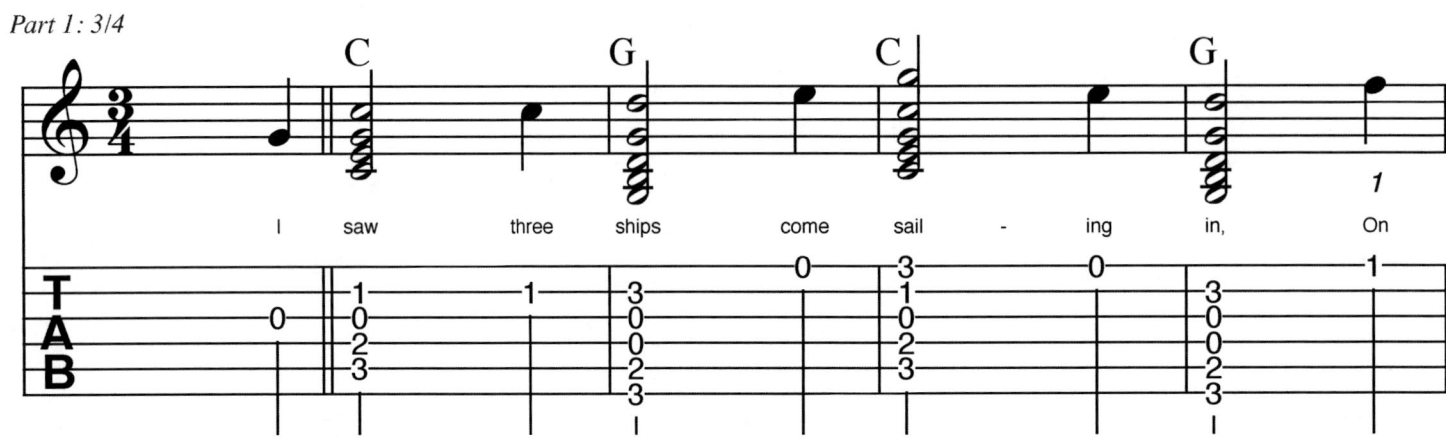

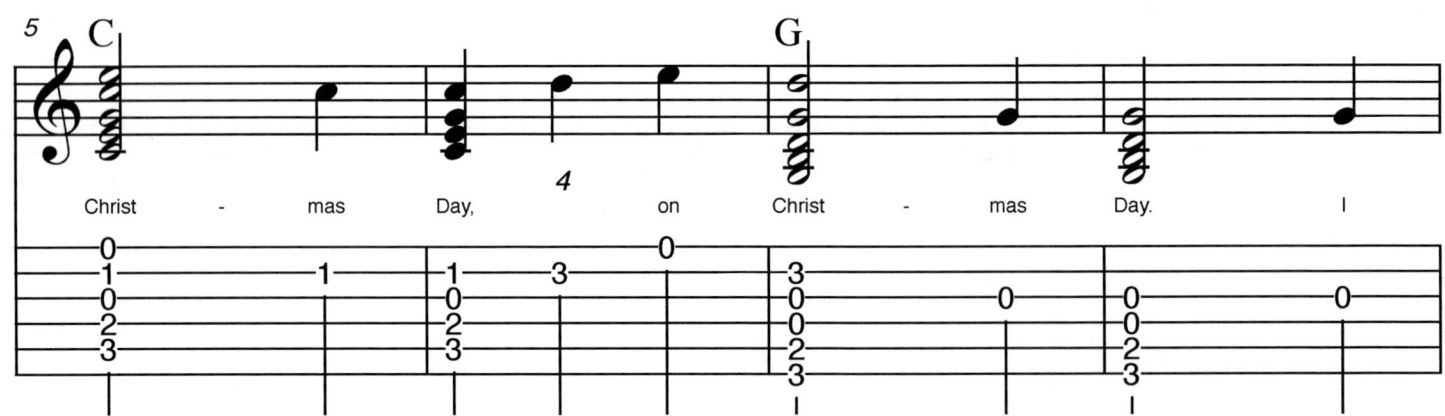

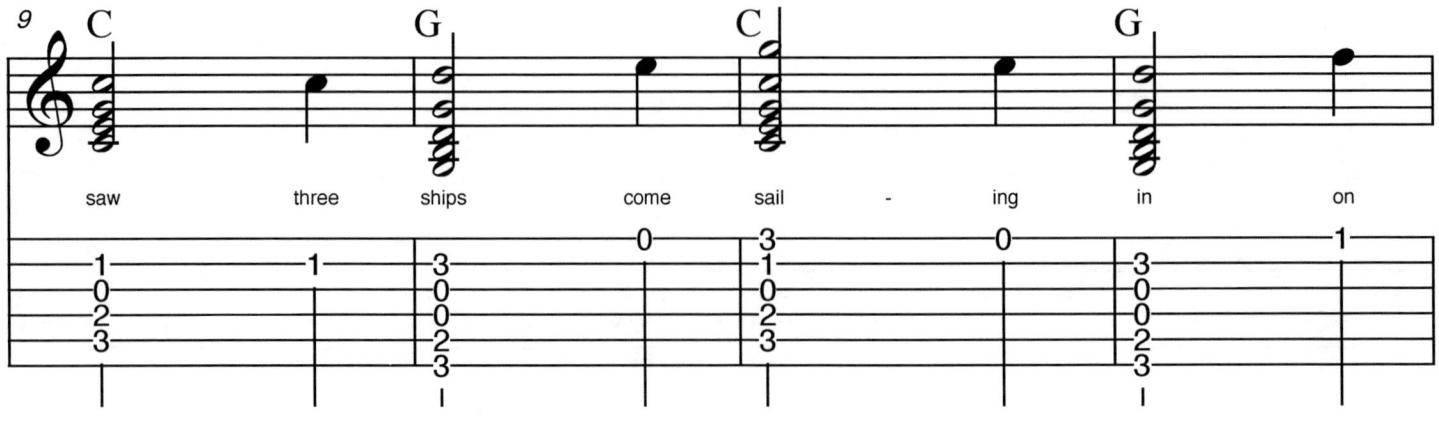

Arrangement copyright © 2009 by Dix Bruce

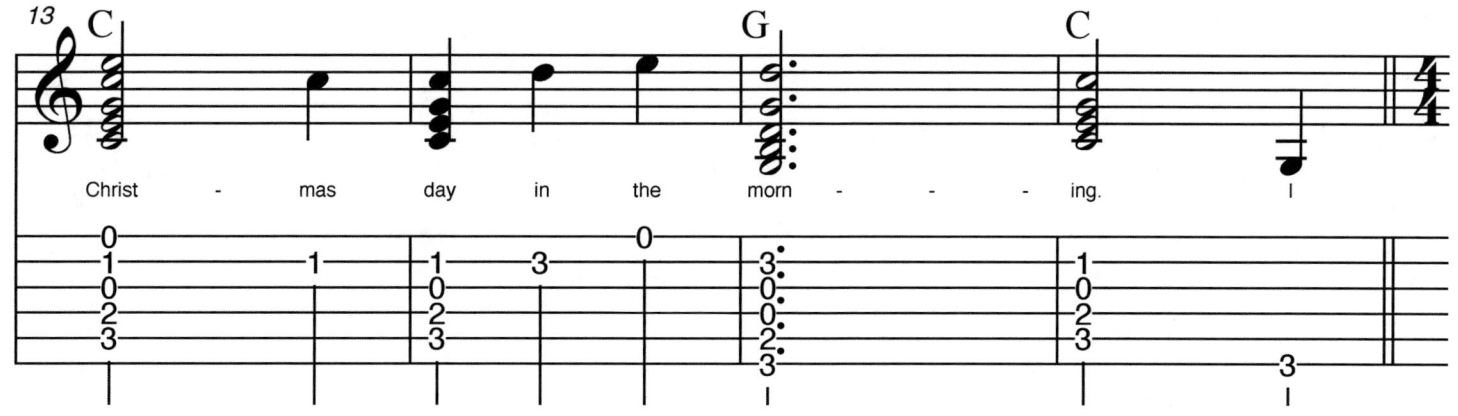

Part 2: 4/4

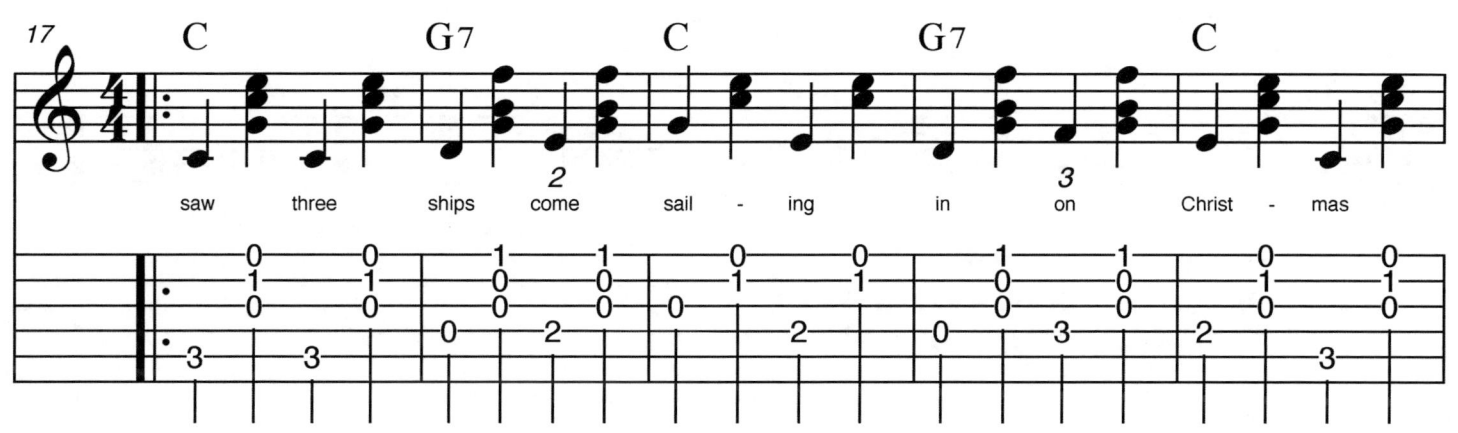

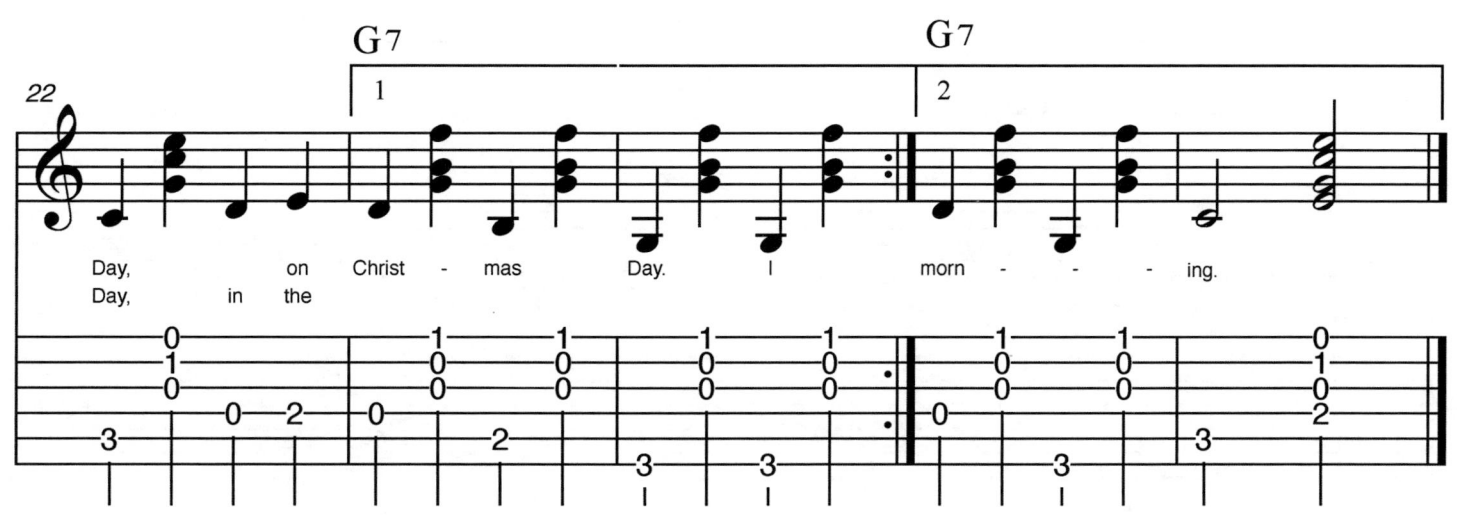

Toyland

M: F, capo 5, F: C or D, capo 0 or 2, CD Tracks 42 & 43

Herbert and MacDonough, 1903

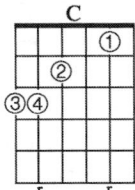 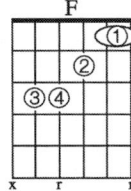 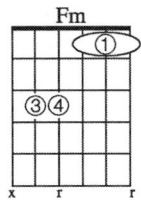 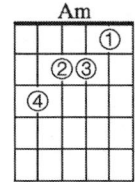

"Toyland" is another beautiful and bittersweet waltz. I put a bluegrass guitar run in the fifteenth measure and also added an extra measure at twenty eight to simulate the ritard that this song is typically performed with. The C chord at left is used in measure eight and twenty four. The F and Fm in nine and ten respectively. You'll use the Am in measure twenty five.

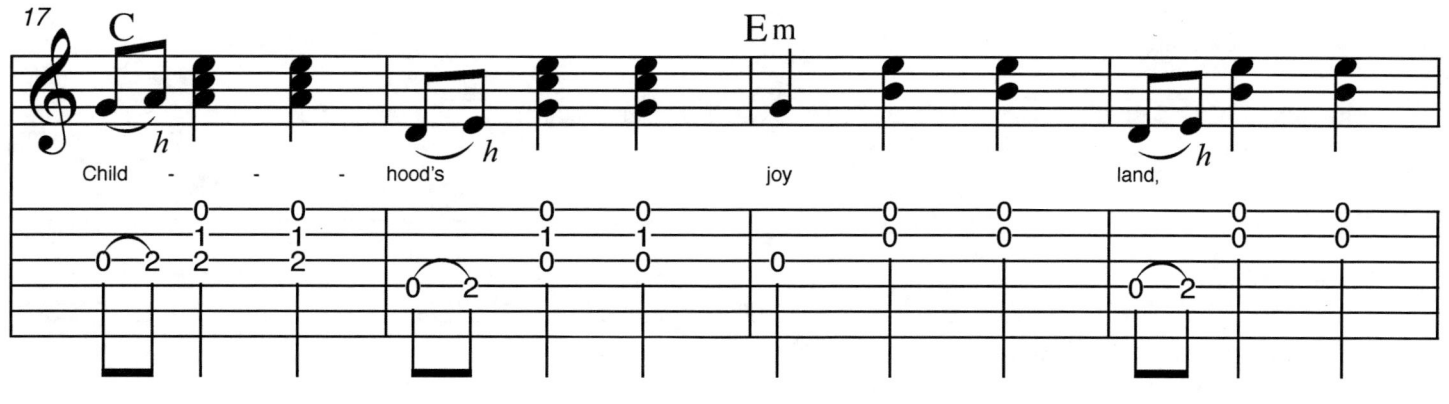

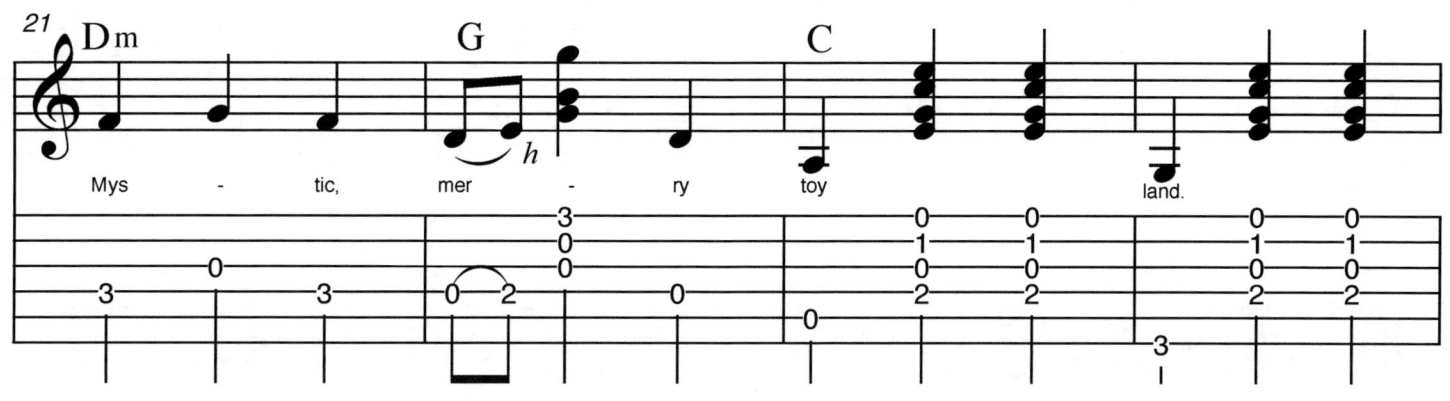

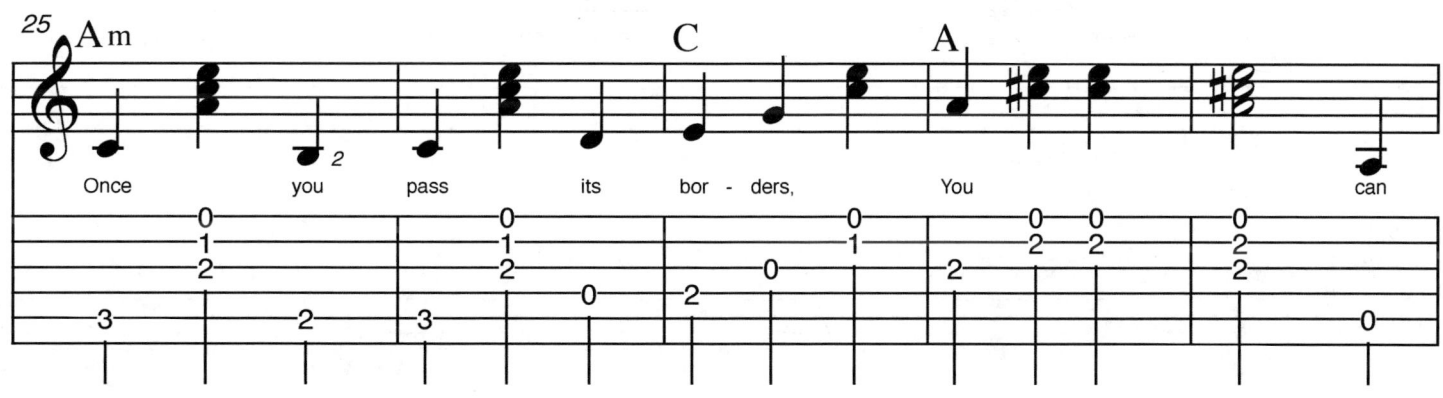

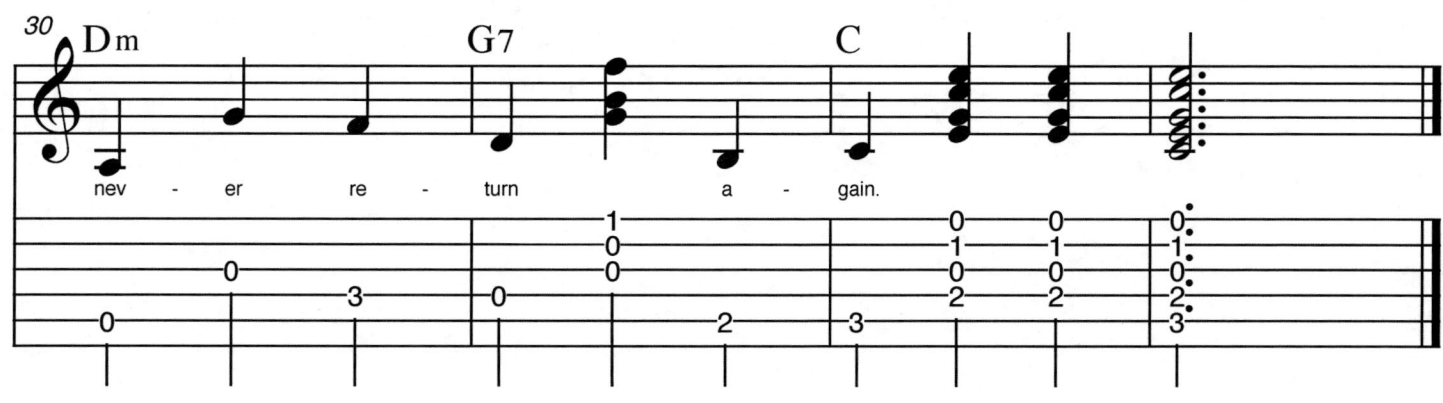

God Rest Ye Merry, Gentlemen

M: Em, F: Am or Bm, capo 5 or 7, CD Tracks 44 & 45

Traditional English Carol, 19the century

Not many strums in "God Rest Ye Merry, Gentlemen" since the melody is made up mostly of quarter notes. Try arpeggio strums in measures six through nine on the first and third beats.

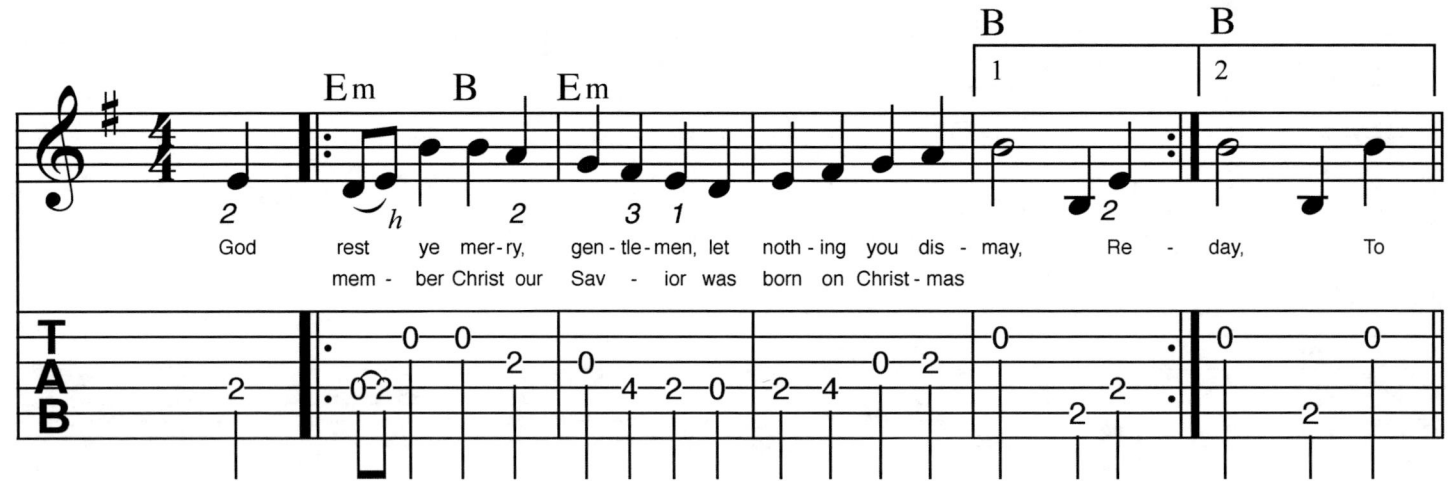

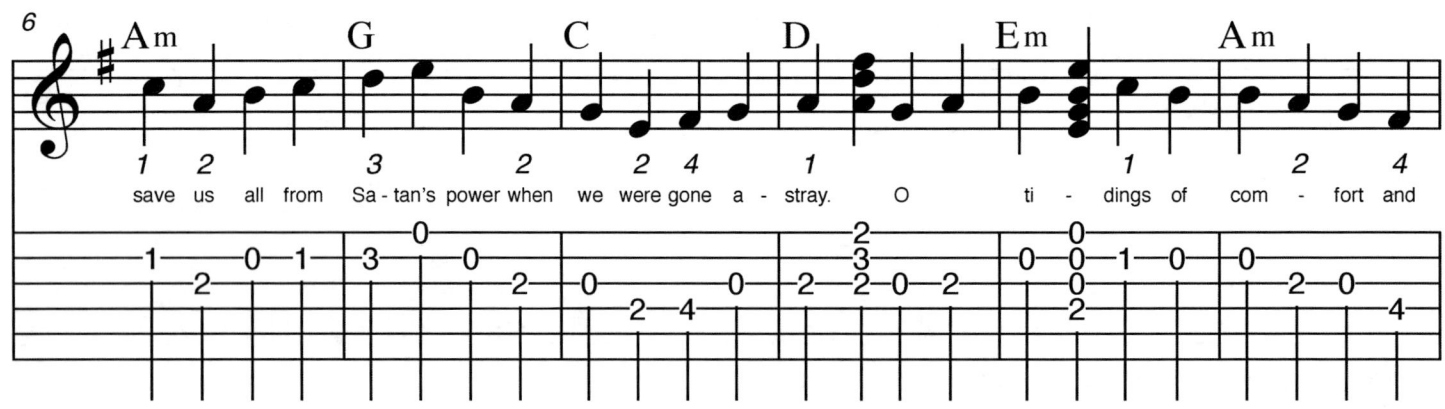

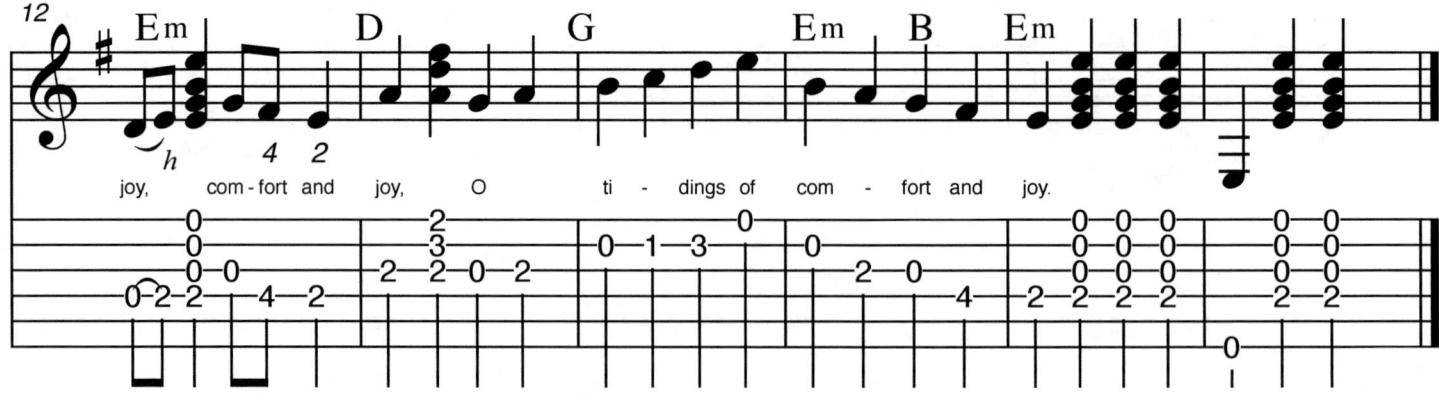

The Friendly Beasts

M: F, F: Bb or C, capo 5 or 7, CD Tracks 46 & 47

Traditional

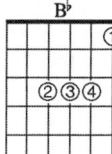

"The Friendly Beasts" has been widely recorded by artists ranging from country and bluegrass to pop under several different titles including "The Donkey Carol" and "The Animal Carol." Don't let the key of F scare you, it works great on this song. Use the Bb at left in measures six and ten. Once you can play it as written, try moving it "over" one string to the key of C so your first note is the third fret, fifth string C.

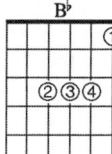

What Child is This?

*M: Dm, capo 5, **F**: Am or Bm, capo 0 or 2, CD Tracks 48 & 49*

English Air, W.C. Dix, 1865

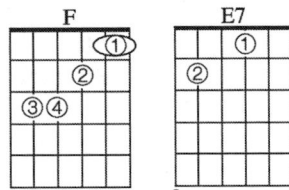

"What Child Is This?" has the same basic melody as "Greensleeves." Notice the eighth note or down-up strums. Try playing other songs in this book with both single quarter note strums and double eighth note strums. Try composing an arpeggio strum version of "What Child Is This?" in either Am or a related key like Em or Dm. The F chord shown at left shows up for the first time in measure five. The E7 appears in measure seven. The familiar extended Am chord with the fourth finger added is used in measure one.

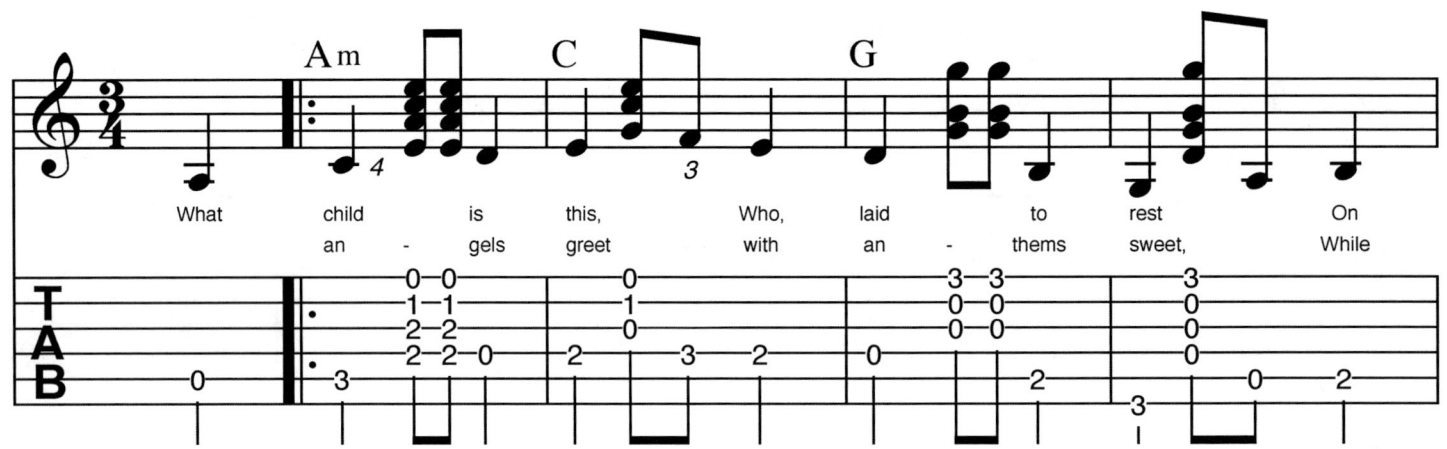

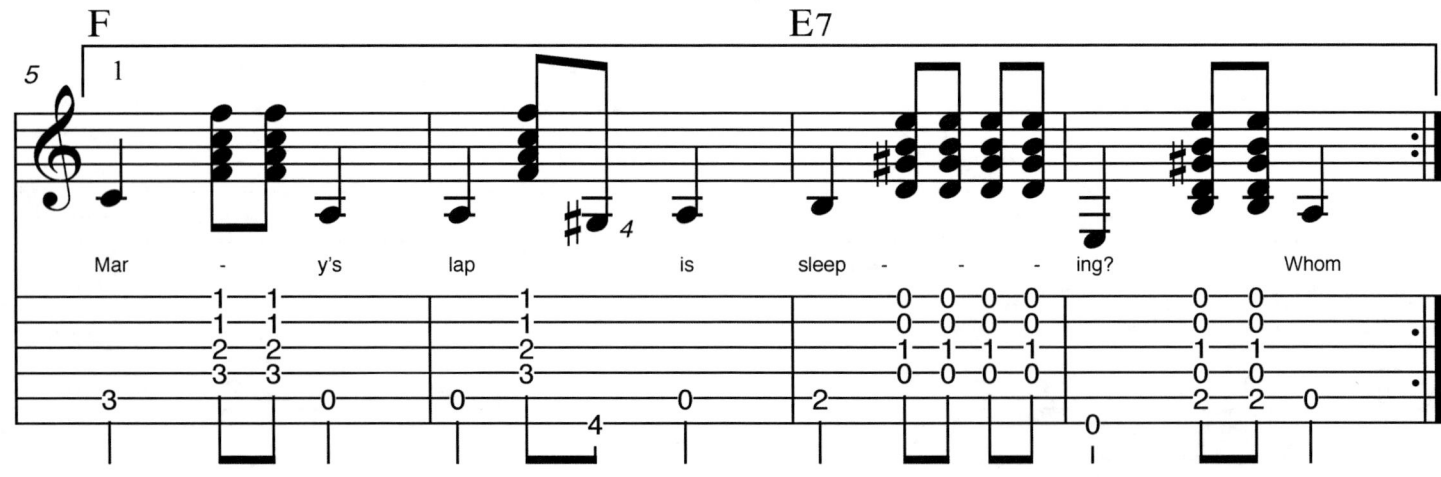

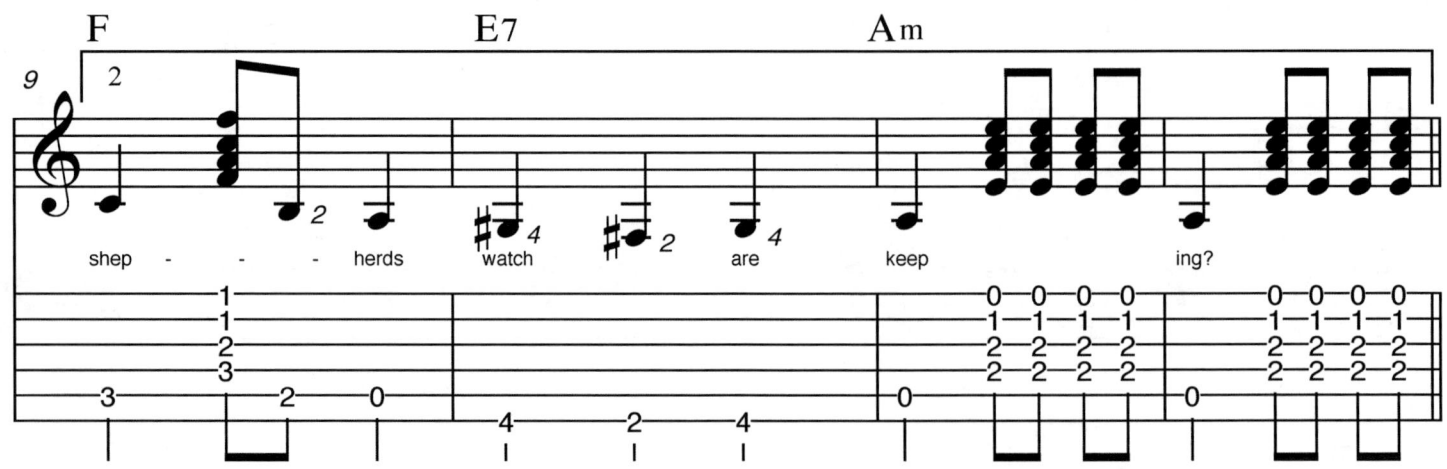

Arrangement copyright © 2009 by Dix Bruce

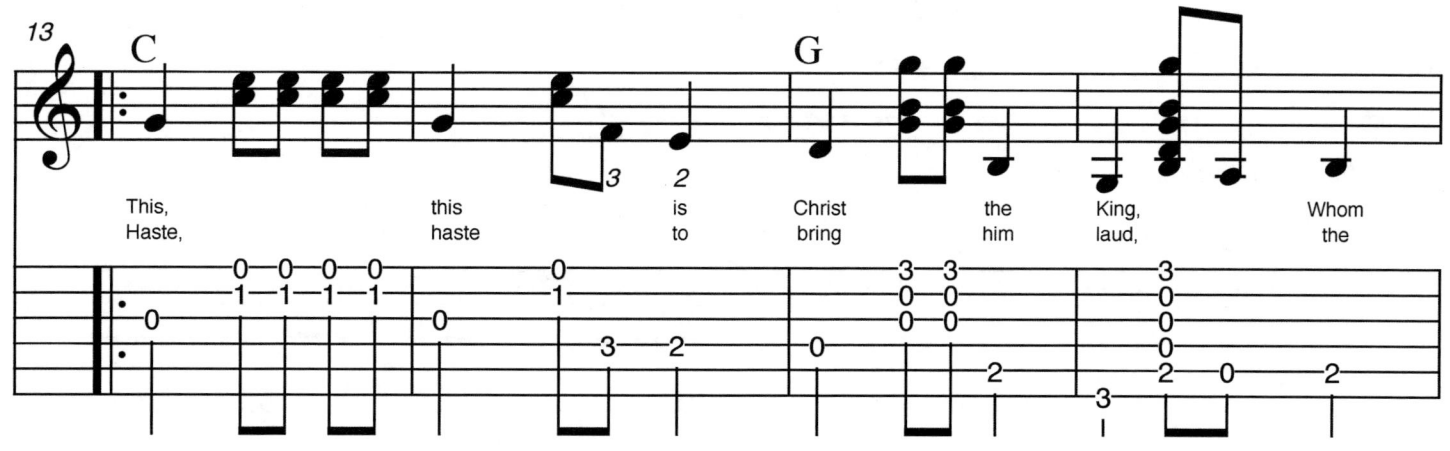

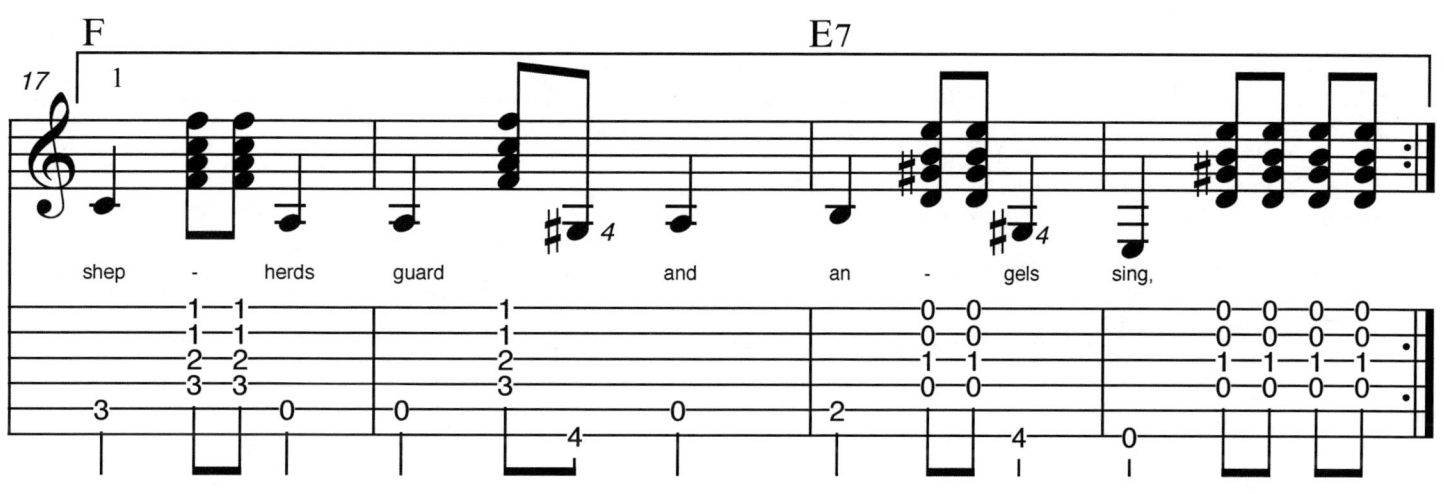

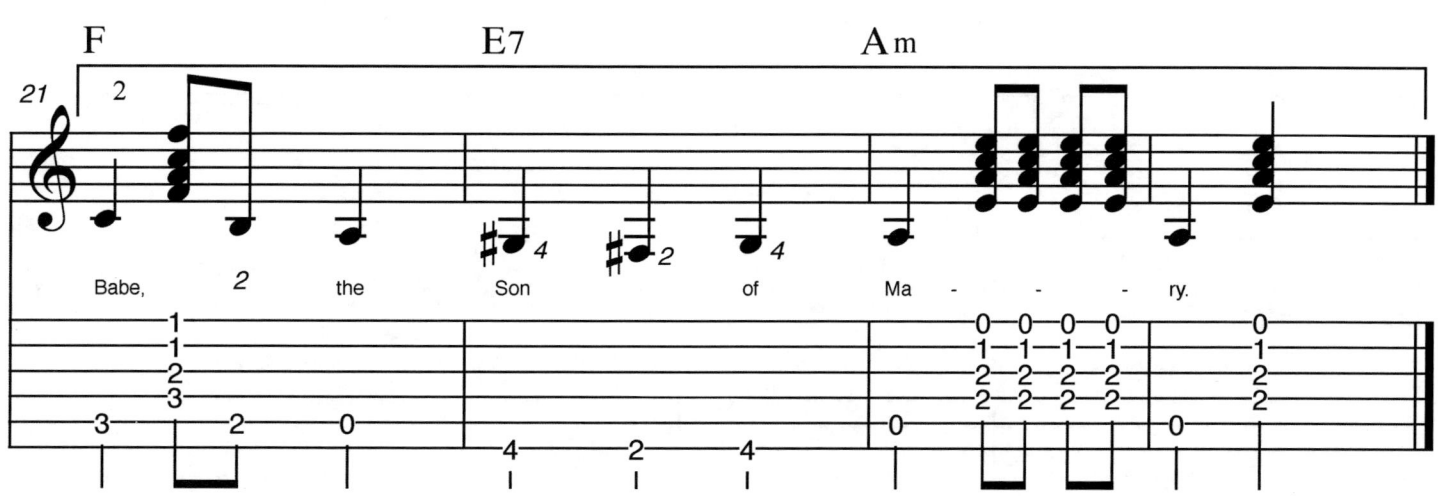

Up on the Housetop

M: C, capo 5, F: G or A, capo 0 or 2, CD Tracks 50 & 51

B.R. Hanby, 1864

This arrangement of "Up on the Housetop" is in two keys and it demonstrates the concept of moving a melody "over" one string to change the key, in this case from the key of G to the key of C.

Arrangement copyright © 2009 by Dix Bruce

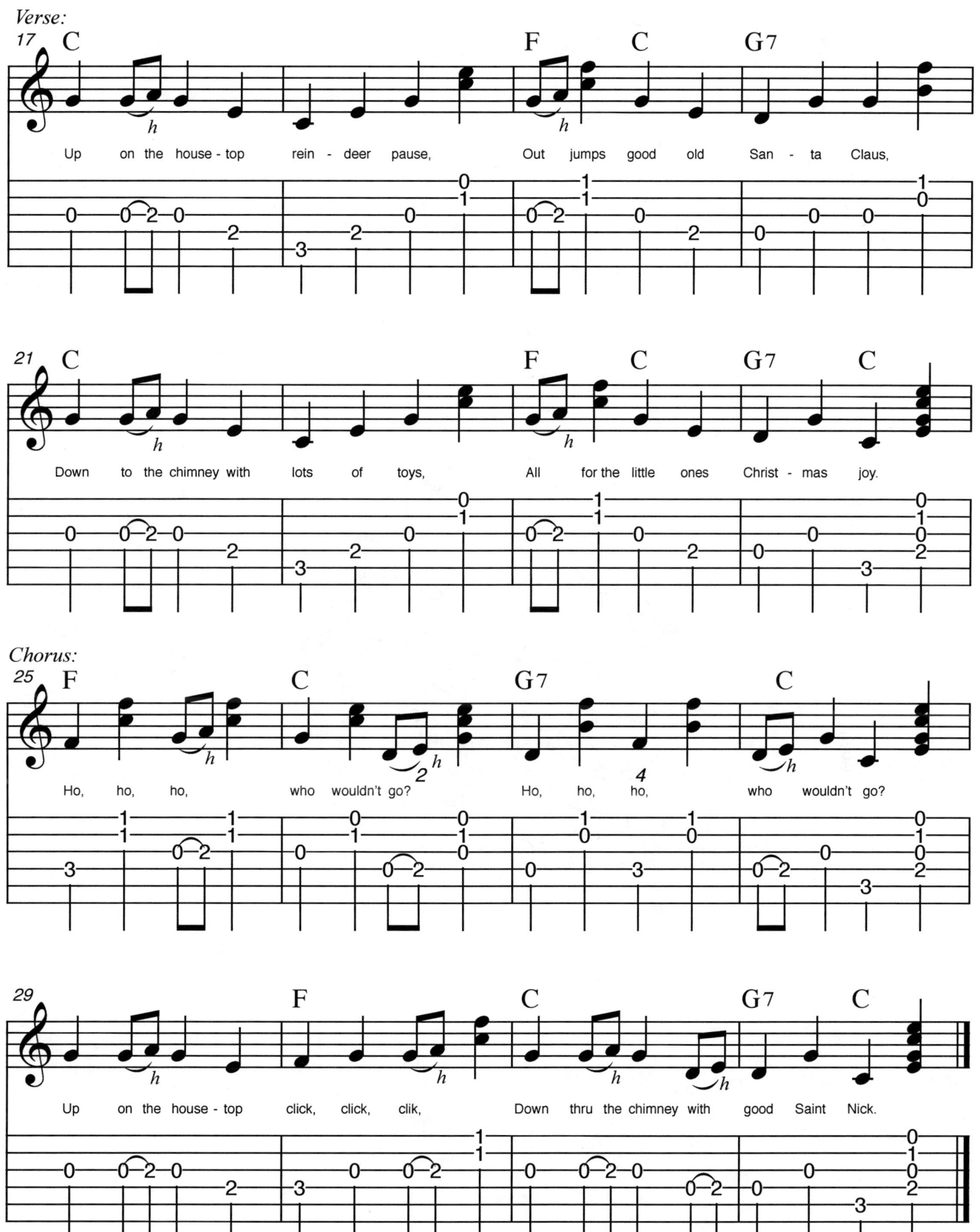

O Holy Night

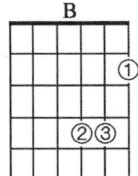
B

Am

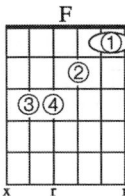
F

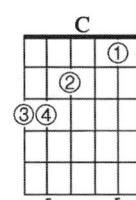
C

"O Holy Night" is not difficult, it just goes through a variety of changes over its considerable length. The most challenging part will probably be turning the page! It's an epic song with lots of tonality changes, hammers, and an octave change in the melody in measure thirty eight.

Don't be spooked by the length of "O Holy Night. Take it a part at a time, for example, first work on measures one through nineteen, then twenty through twenty seven, then twenty eight through thirty seven, then thirty eight through sixty, then sixty through the end. It's a stunning song and well worth the effort.

Use the B in measures twenty three and twenty four, the Am in measure thirty eight, the F in measure sixty, the C in measure seventy nine.

Try adding hammer-ons to the E notes in measures seventy four through seventy six.

O Holy Night

M: G, capo 7, F: C or D, capo 0 or 2, CD Tracks 52 & 53

Adam, 1847

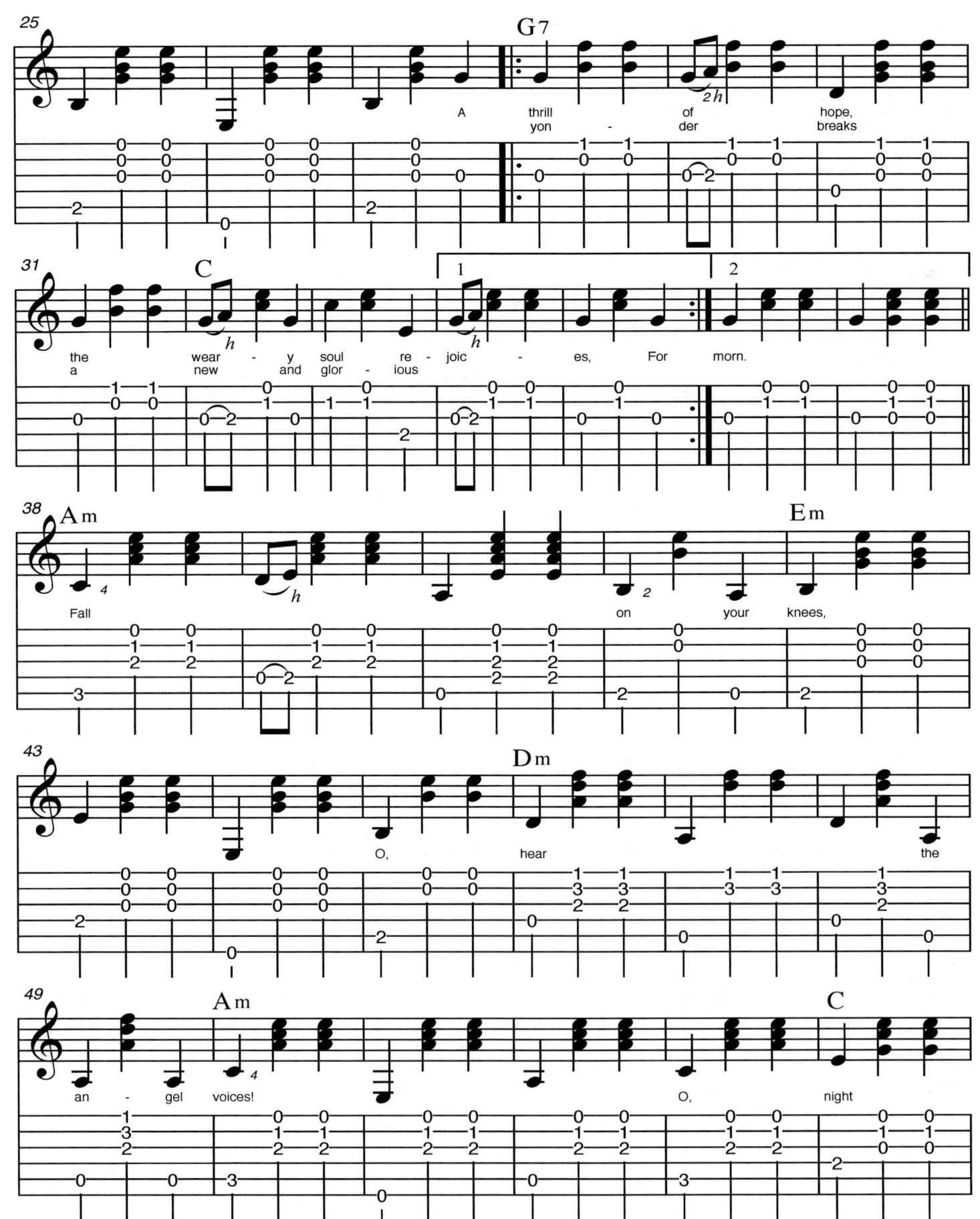

We Three Kings of Orient Are

M: Dm, capo 5, F: Am or Bm, capo 0 or 2, CD Tracks 54 & 55

Hopkins, 1857

Notice the *fermata* or hold in measure fourteen. It comes right after the "oh, oh" and before the "Star of wonder" lyrics. I hold the chord for about six beats. You can add a *ritard* or gradual slow down in the measure before it. Play it as you feel it.

If you play the arrangement more than once, add an E7 chord in measure thirty one to bring you back to the Am at the beginning. Last time through play a C chord to end. I didn't include any hammer-ons in this arrangement but there's no reason you couldn't add a few. Try playing them in measure one, seven, and other likely locations. "We Three Kings" is another good one to move over a string and transpose to other keys like Dm and Em. Try moving it on your own first but if you get stuck, you can download the music from my website: http://www.musixnow.com/christmasguitardownloads.html.

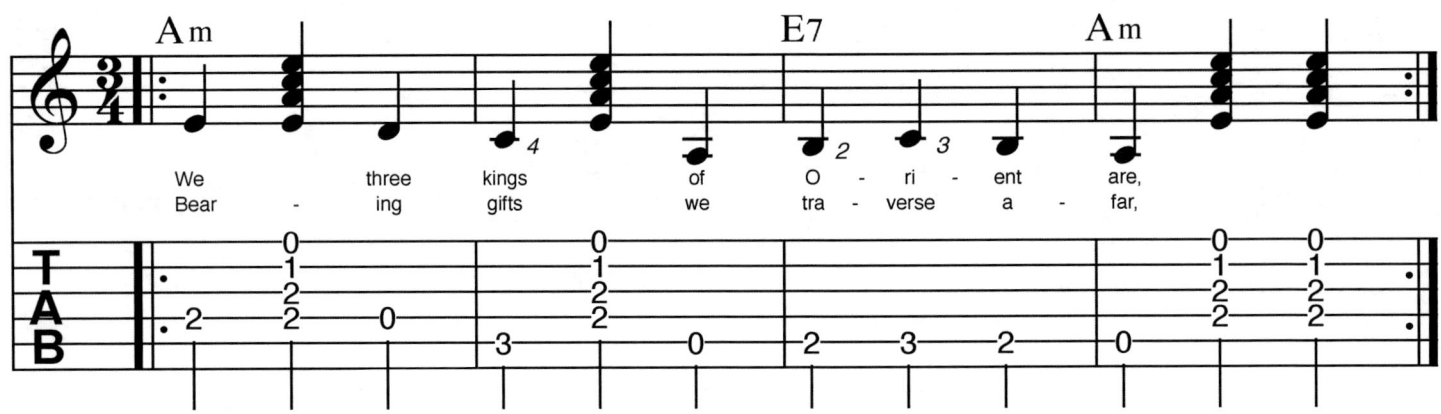

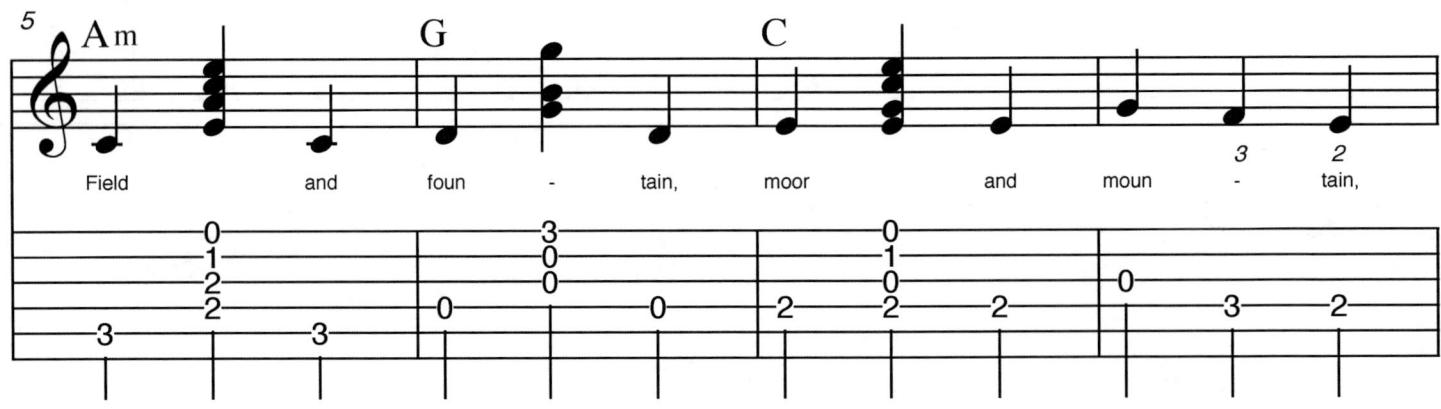

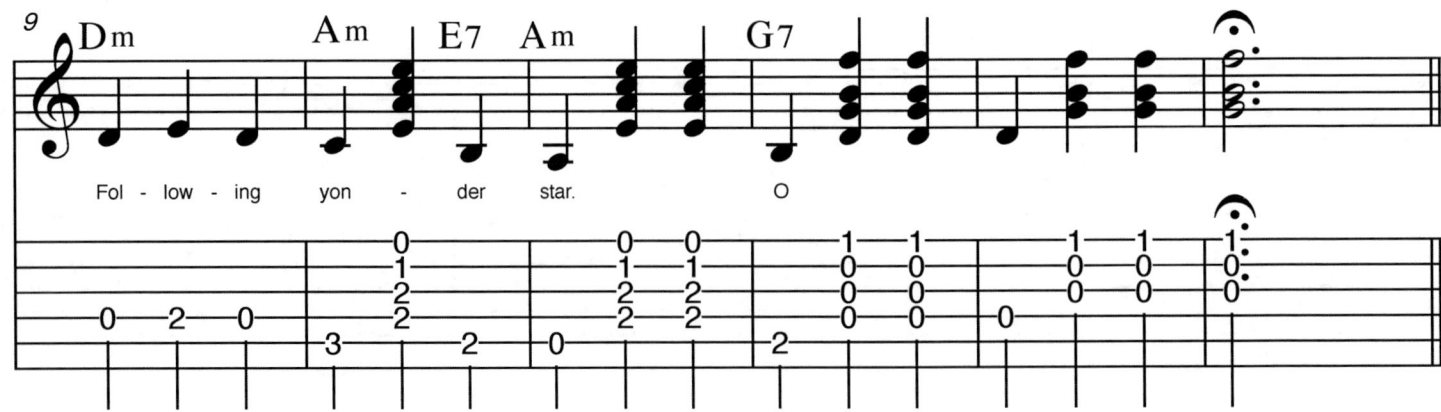

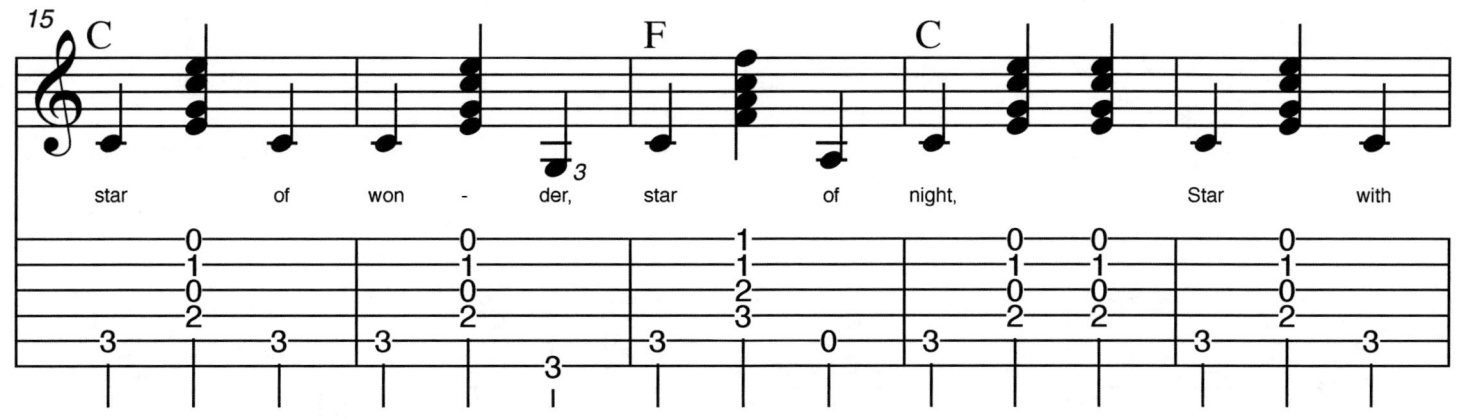

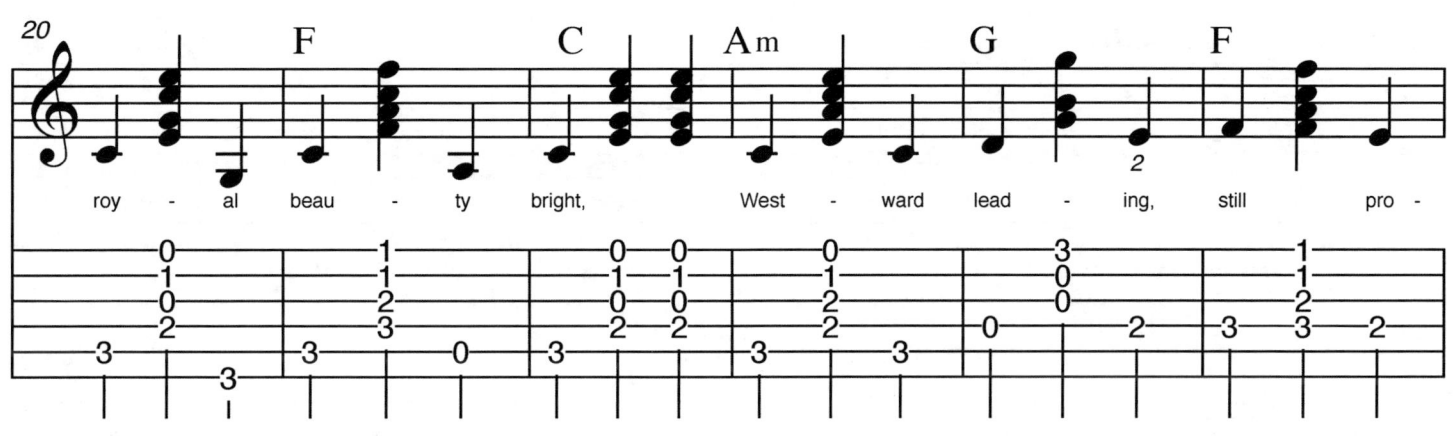

If repeated,
play an E7 here.

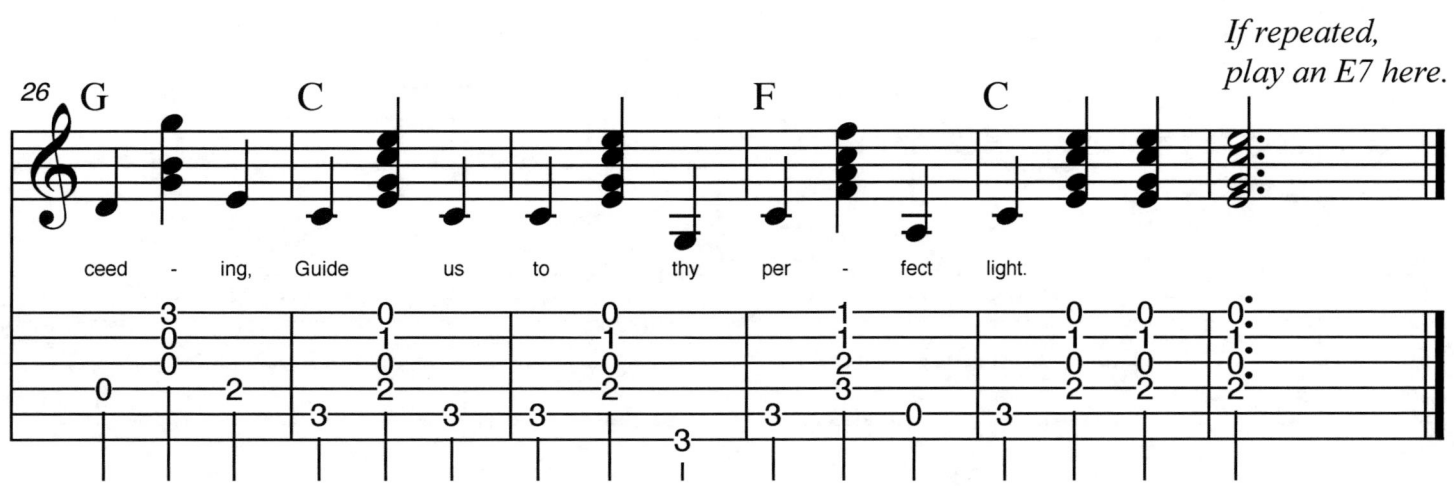

It Came Upon the Midnight Clear

M: G, capo 7, F: C or D, capo 0 or 2, CD Tracks 56 & 57

Sears, Willis, 19th century

The many hammer-ons in "It Came Upon the Midnight Clear" help give this wonderful waltz it's dreamy, almost jazzy feel. You'll slowly arpeggiate the G7 chord in measure twelve and clearly sound each note in the chord. Try moving the whole arrangement "over" one string to the key of F. Your first note will be on the third fret, fifth string C.

The Coventry Carol

This arrangement of "The Coventry Carol" will take you through three keys, Em, Am, and Dm. There are some difficult parts here and there but working through all three keys will give you great practice with moving melodies and solos from one key to another. Try this same kind of shifting around with the other songs in the book.

"The Coventry Carol" should be played slowly. It's tone is sombre, quiet and dark. Isn't it interesting how the tonality shifts from minor to major in the last two measures of each key/page?

Vocal keys are listed on the next page without capo numbers since the three keys should accommodate just about any voice.

Use the D chord below in measure three, the B7 in four, the Am in eleven on page fifty. Use the G chord in measure twenty five, the Dm in twenty seven on page fifty one. Use the Am in measure thirty six, the Gm in thirty eight on page fifty two.

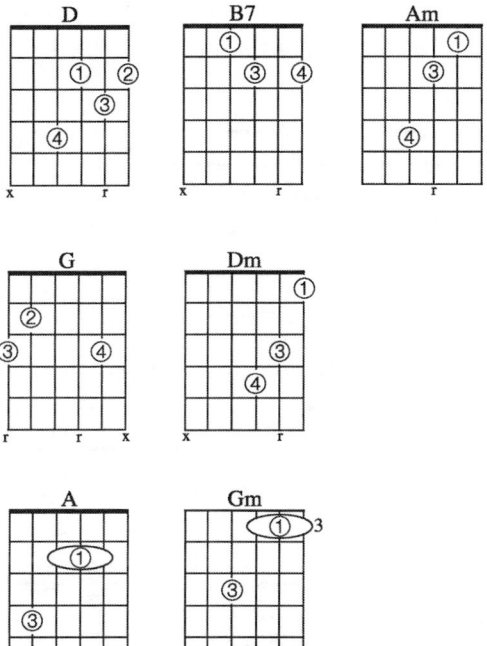

The Coventry Carol

M: Gm, F: Cm or Dm, CD Tracks 58 & 59

English, 16 century

Books and instructional DVDs by Dix Bruce

(For complete details, as well as info on new books, CDs and DVDs, contact www. musixnow.com)

The Parking Lot Picker's Songbooks Guitar, Mandolin, Fiddle (with Gerald Jones), Dobro (with Stacy Phillips), Bass, & Banjo (with Bill Evans).

You Can Teach Yourself Country Guitar book & CD, DVD, or video set.

You Can Teach Yourself Mandolin book & CD, DV,D or video set.

Getting into Bluegrass Mandolin book & CD.

Gypsy Swing & Hot Club Rhythm, Vol. 1. Separate editions for Guitar and Mandolin. Learn chords and practice melodies and soloing on 12 great songs while playing along with a great Hot Club Band.

Gypsy Swing & Hot Club Rhythm, Vol. 2. Learn 12 more great songs in the Gypsy Swing/Hot Club style.

First Lessons Mandolin book, CD, & DVD set.

BackUp Trax: Old Time Fiddle Tunes Vol. I book & CD set. Jam all night long with the band on old time and fiddle tunes.

BackUp Trax: Swing & Jazz Vol. I book & CD set. Jam all night long with a great band. You play all the leads and the band never gets tired!

BackUp Trax: Traditional Jazz & Dixieland book & CD set. Jam all night long with the band on the basic Dixieland repertoire.

BackUp Trax: Early Jazz & Hot Tunes book & CD set. Jam all night long with the band on more traditional jazz standards.

Basic Swing Guitar (DVD). Learn swing chord comping on the classics of the genre.

Basic Country Flatpicking Guitar (DVD). Explores easy Carter-style solos.

Recordings:

Brothers at Heart by Dix Bruce & Jim Nunally. Brother duet-style songs, & hot guitar picking (FGM CD 111).

From Fathers to Sons by Dix Bruce & Jim Nunally. Folk, bluegrass, & hot guitar picking (Musix CD/C 104).

In My Beautiful Dream by Dix Bruce & Jim Nunally. Great new songs & old classics by the duo. (Musix CD 106).

The Way Things Are by Dix Bruce & Jim Nunally. More hot picking & great new songs by the duo.
My Folk Heart by Dix Bruce, solo & small group, traditional American folk music (Musix CD/C101).
With Jim Nunally, Tom Rozum, and John Reischman.

Tuxedo Blues by Dix Bruce, string swing & jazz (Musix CD/C102). With Bob Alekno on mandolin, David Balakrishnan on violin, and Mike Wollenberg on bass.

Auld Lang Syne

M: D, F: G or A, capo 5 or 7, CD Tracks 60 & 61

R. Burns, Scottish, 1788

"Auld Lang Syne" is a "must-know" for musicians of every style. Otherwise, you might just as well stay home on New Years! This arrangement includes a very bluegrassy bass run in measures fifteen and thirty one. The chords in parenthesis (Bm), (G), are optional and add a little extra spice to the accompaniment. Give the G chord strums a little extra accent on measures sixteen and twenty. Drag the chord out and sound the top note, the second string B note, more prominently than the others.

Index